Dear Reader:

The book you are about to read is the latest bestseller from St. Martin's True Crime Library, the imprint *The New York Times* calls "the leader in true crime!" Each month, we offer you a fascinating account of the latest, most sensational crime that has captured the national attention. *The Milwaukee Murders* delves into the twisted world of Jeffrey Dahmer, one of the most savage serial killers of our time; *Lethal Lolita* gives you the *real* scoop on the deadly love affair between Amy Fisher and Joey Buttafuoco; *Whoever Fights Monsters* takes you inside the special FBI team that tracks serial killers; *Garden of Graves* reveals how police uncovered the bloody human harvest of mass murderer Joel Rifkin; *Unanswered Cries* is the story of a detective who tracked a killer for a year, only to discover it was someone he knew and trusted; *Bad Blood* is the story of the notorious Menendez brothers and their sensational trials; *Sins of the Mother* details the sad account of Susan Smith and her two drowned children; *Fallen Hero* details the riveting tragedy of O. J. Simpson and the case that stunned a nation.

St. Martin's True Crime Library gives you the stories *behind* the headlines. Our authors take you right to the scene of the crime and into the minds of the most notorious murderers to show you what really makes them tick. St. Martin's True Crime Library paperbacks are better than the most terrifying thriller, because it's all true! The next time you want a crackling good read, make sure it's got the St. Martin's True Crime Library logo on the spine—you'll be up all night!

Charles E. Spicer, Jr.
Senior Editor, St. Martin's True Crime Library

"He's hurting me!" Marie yelled, as Jed put his hands around her throat. "Somebody help me!"

One first-floor tenant of the building, Michael Menard, could not simply roll over and ignore Marie's pleas for help. He got up from his bed, opened his apartment door, and saw Jed grab Marie around the neck with both hands. "You better let her go!" Menard said in a menacing voice, and went back into his apartment to fetch a baseball bat. Meanwhile, his girlfriend Lisa had called the police.

Jed tried to drag Marie back upstairs, while she continued yelling: "Help me! He's hurting me! Stop hurting me!"

By the time the police arrived, Jed had fled the scene. One of the policemen asked her if she wanted him arrested.

"No," she said. It was probably the biggest mistake of her young life.

LIKE MOTHER, LIKE SON

William G. Flanagan

St. Martin's Paperbacks

LIKE MOTHER, LIKE SON

ISBN: 0-312-95643-6

Printed in the United States of America

St. Martin's Paperbacks edition/December 1995

10 9 8 7 6 5 4 3 2 1

In memory of my dad, William G. Flanagan, formerly an NYPD detective with the district attorney's office in Manhattan.

Dialogue and thoughts have been reconstructed based on testimony and interviews.

1

The Grand Hyatt Hotel on New York's storied 42nd Street had always been good luck to 34-year-old Jed Ardito. It was the logical place to book a room on April 28, 1993, for what he hoped would be a very special afternoon with the love of his life, Marie Daniele.

Despite all the troubles they'd had over their stormy four-year relationship, Jed wanted to bury the past and start anew. He now knew for sure what he wanted most in life—Marie. Actually, he had known it for a long time. But he had blown it before, when she was so ready and willing to become his wife.

He had to convince her that this time he would not disappoint her. That this time they really would get married, have kids, and share a great life together.

But Marie would now need a lot of convincing. Before, when they were engaged, it was Jed himself who had his doubts. It was Jed who walked out on her. It was Jed who suddenly ran off and married someone else. It was Jed who left Marie alone to face her stunned parents and friends.

Now the tables had turned.

Now Marie, his precious Marie, who had always needed him and wanted him and loved him like no one before or since, was slipping away from him. And he couldn't let that happen. Despite what his friends advised him, and what Marie's friends and family had advised her, Jed knew that they could be happy together. They didn't know Marie the way he did. They didn't know the very special relationship they shared; the things they did together; the special magic of their lovemaking. He wouldn't let her go. He couldn't.

But 24-year-old Marie Daniele had reached a turning point in her long, mercurial love affair with Jed.

"I want to get on with my life," she'd told Cara Levinson, her best friend, just a few days before. She had known Cara for only a few years, but they had become friends right from the start, and were now best friends. In Cara's words, as soon as they met, they "just clicked."

It was easy to see why. Both women were attractive, confident, and well on their way to becoming successful. And they both attracted men easily.

They had gone to a nail salon to have their nails done together. And, of course, to talk. And they talked about a lot of things, not just Jed, the way it had been so often before.

Cara felt good about Marie finally coming to her senses. As her closest friend, Cara knew that there was something destructive and dangerous about that relationship. It was so good to hear Marie talk of other things, and other people besides Jed.

"There's someone new I met," Marie confided to Cara. "A really nice guy. Named Michael."

Finally, Cara thought. "Is he someone who respects you, and treats you like you should be treated?"

Marie flashed a big smile, and Cara smiled too. She felt relieved and happy for her friend. Cara had never made any secret of her dislike of Jed. He had hurt her dearest friend and the quicker Marie was rid of him the better.

But everyone who knew Jed and Marie also knew that their relationship would not die easily, or peacefully. There was lots of love there—perhaps too much. But there was also plenty of hurt and anger and resentment.

In a way, they were lovers who had been married for many stormy years, and were now going through a bitter and vindictive divorce—which both were afraid of. They feared the peace and boredom that might result.

But Marie had passed the point of no return with Jed. She was not quite ready to stop seeing him completely, but she was determined to one day be free of him.

Marie had made her feelings known to Jed, by both actions and words. After all, hadn't she returned from a solo trip to Florida, to get an early start on her summer tan? A tan that wouldn't be for Jed's benefit.

Jed did not take kindly to Marie's wanting to break up. He had discussed Marie often with a woman friend of his, Denise Marshall, whom he'd met through business six years earlier. Denise had known Marie a long time, too, and knew how destructive their relationship had been. She also knew that Marie had reached a decision about Jed.

"She wanted to break up, but he didn't want it to happen," Denise would later say. "He told me that three or four times that month. He said she had called him many times to say she wanted to break up. But he did not want to stop seeing her."

As she had done in the past, Denise urged him to forget about Marie.

But Jed refused to go quietly into the night. The more Marie talked breakup, the more he talked marriage. After all, earlier in their relationship, wasn't marriage what she'd always wanted? As far as Jed was concerned, Marie was now just calling his bluff. What he didn't seem able to grasp was that things had changed. Marie didn't want him on any terms anymore.

Only a few Sundays before that fateful Wednesday afternoon of April 28, 1993, Jed had spent the afternoon with the Goldsteins in their house up in Westchester. Eric Goldstein was Jed's boss, and perhaps his closest friend. Eric had even named his son after Jed, despite the fact that it went against Goldstein's religion to name a child after someone who was still living.

As Jed and Eric talked that Sunday, the subject of Marie came up again, as it inevitably did. "I'm determined to marry her," Jed said.

Eric sighed. He'd had a ringside seat to their torturous romance right from the beginning. At times, when the hopelessness of the relationship was apparent to everyone but Jed and Marie, Eric had done what he could to break them up. He had encouraged Jed to marry Petra,* and once he did, he thought that would be the end of Marie. He had fired Marie from the business that he and Jed then ran together; Eric didn't want her around to tempt Jed after he had married Petra. Eric had heard it all before.

"But she doesn't want to marry you, Jed, does she? Come on, let it go," he urged him.

But Jed ignored Eric too. He ignored everyone when it came to Marie. No one knew Marie—really knew her— the way Jed did. He knew that in her heart of hearts she loved him the way she could love no one else. They were addicted to one another—and he would do whatever was necessary to see that they would always be in one another's lives.

*Not her real name.

* * *

The Grand Hyatt held good memories for both Jed and Marie. In happier moments, they used to have lunch there, at the Sun Garden Grill, stealing time from their busy schedules.

Few couples would find anything romantic about the Grand Hyatt. It's a 1,200-room, behemoth of a hotel, which throbs with business travelers, conventioneers wearing plastic name tags, and tour groups clustered over their luggage like bees around a hive.

Under its four-story atrium, the length and width of a football field, are groves of potted plants and an incongruous two-story waterfall that barely manages to drown out the cacophony of street noise that leaks in from the street. Everywhere there is glass and brass and shiny marble surfaces. The scene looks more like an Atlantic City casino than a hotel; co-owner Donald Trump had left his indelible mark. It is hard and glitzy and impersonal, a place to rush through.

But Jed loved the Grand Hyatt. For one thing, it was handy. His business—suppling temporary office workers to companies with the occasional need for additional secretarial and computer help—meant that he had to be near Grand Central Station, which is right under the Hyatt. Many temporary-help agencies are clustered in the area— Grand Central is easy to reach for the thousands of secretaries, clerks, typists, and computer operators who are forced to, or who chose to, work as "temps." Most subway lines connect here. And the Metro North lines from Westchester and Connecticut terminate here. Grand Central, and the Hyatt, were ground zero for Jed Ardito. It was where the action was.

Jed often entertained clients in the Hyatt's restaurants and the glassed-in bar overhanging the bustle of 42nd Street. He used it for many important occasions. And

April 28, 1993, was a very important occasion. It was the day he hoped to win Marie back for good.

Jed was feeling pretty good about himself that spring day. He was arranging to sublease on a new apartment in midtown, one that he was sure Marie would love. He knew, of course, that she would never go back to his other apartment at 336 West 49th Street—not after that horrible night two months before. But he didn't want to think about that night now. Or ever again. That was all part of the past that was to be expunged from their lives. That night had been just a bad dream, a nightmare that didn't really happen. He hadn't been himself that night— and neither had Marie. No, it wasn't real. That cold, crazy night in February hadn't really happened at all. There had been no horrible fight in the lobby of the apartment building, no alarmed neighbors, no neighbor brandishing a baseball bat, no 911 call to the police, no frantic escape into the dark night. No. That was all a fantasy born of the cold, dark winter.

Now it was spring again—a very promising spring. And a busy one for Jed and Marie. It was a busy time in the office-temp business, as companies that laid off employees before Christmas now had to turn to temps to fill the gap. Jed knew that Eric was expecting a lot of him in the months ahead, but he knew he could produce. For when he was on his game, he was as good as they come. "The best salesman in New York," Eric had called him. And Eric, as Jed knew all too well, was first and foremost a businessman who didn't lavish praise.

Yes, damn it, Jed was good. He trafficked in office temporaries the way a cattle-dealer supplies steers. Success rests not so much in finding animals for slaughter, but in getting contracts from slaughterhouses for the steers. And Jed had learned early the two best ways of getting beefy contracts for temporaries: one, by wining and dining, and occasionally wooing whoever it was who awarded those contracts; and two, by hiring away from other temporary-help agencies the best salespeople, ones who had their clients' allegiances and could take their business with them.

It was a profession for which Jed Ardito was well suited. He knew how to charm, flatter, and manipulate—especially women. And stealth was ingrained in him. Those traits worked better for him than trying to write winning pitch letters, or make boffo presentations to clients. Eric Goldstein could take care of the administration and the paperwork; Jed could handle the people end.

It was through his office-temp business that Jed had first met Marie Daniele, four years earlier, in 1989. She was just a kid then, barely 19, her teeth in braces. She was a little unsure of herself, but Jed saw she had drive and street smarts and a sense of humor. Jed had heard about how well she was doing for a competitor, and so decided to lure her—and hopefully her clients—to Temp-Rite, the agency which he then co-owned with Goldstein.

Marie proved to be a very good hire. After a while, she also proved to be the best lover, and the most important person, in Jed's life. She still was—even after four years and all the pain and embarrassment he had caused her.

It was not quite 10 o'clock that cool Wednesday when Jed stood at the desk of the Grand Hyatt to reserve a room upstairs.

He smiled at the reservations clerk, an attractive, young Asian-American woman with dark, almond-shaped eyes. Jed explained that he wanted to check in early, long before the normal check-in time of 1 P. M. He said that he had called the hotel earlier from his office, but had encountered trouble reserving a room for so early in the day.

So he walked over to the hotel from his office, Creative Network Systems, at 295 Madison Avenue, just a few blocks away. He felt he'd have better success in person, wallet in hand. The reservations clerk checked the computer for his name. It showed he had indeed called earlier, requesting the early check-in. There was a notation from whomever he'd spoken to that, if possible, he should be accommodated.

The reservations clerk smiled back at the tall, well-dressed young man with the deep blue eyes, sharp Roman nose, and dark, wavy hair. She checked the room list. There were rooms available. She didn't need to ask why this handsome young man would want a room for so early in the day; especially a man without a suitcase or an out-of-town address. She had been a receptionist a while, had seen quite a few men arrange noontime trysts at the centrally located, anonymous Hyatt.

The clerk found a room for him and smiled sheepishly. Jed's charm had worked again. Despite the rate of $234.54, which he had trouble affording these days, Jed registered in his own name, paid in cash, then walked toward the bank of elevators at the far end of the giant atrium. Then he took the elevator to the top floor, the 34th floor, and walked toward the west wing.

Room 3431 was decent-sized, nicely furnished, and had a king-size bed. It was lot better than some of the other hotels Jed had taken Marie to in recent months.

Jed took off his coat, put down his briefcase, and looked around the room. He hoped Marie would like it. For $235, she had better.

He picked up the phone and called Marie at Viva Temporary Services, 15 East 40th St., the temporary-help agency where she now worked. It was only a few minutes away. He told her he had the room and asked her to meet him there after noon. "We'll have lunch sent up," he told her. "And we can talk." She was very busy, she said, she had a full day planned, but she said she'd come. Why not? She could handle Jed now. She wasn't intimidated by him any longer. She knew that things would never be the way they once were between them. Nor did she want them to be. For a change, Marie was in control of their relationship, the dismantling of it, and she felt very good about that. Jed would just have to realize that yes, maybe they could remain friends, but they had no future together any longer. He would have to face that fact. Only then would he stop his whining, his rambling phone calls, and his talk of marriage. And only then would Marie be finally free of him.

Marie knew that her sister, her friends—and especially her family—would think she was crazy to even see him anymore. But she saw no harm in at least listening to him; she thought it would make him come to his senses faster. And, yes, she had to admit it made her feel good to hurt him a bit for a change. For God knows, he had hurt her more than anything in her young life.

Jed feared that his time with Marie might really be running out. There was a hardness to Marie now he had never seen before. She seemed distracted. She didn't look him in the eyes the way he wanted her to. She was drifting away from him fast.

So he had to be especially nice to her. He squeezed some more time out of his own busy morning to drop into a nearby jewelry shop, to buy her a pearl bracelet with a gold chain. Marie had always loved gifts. Over the years Jed had given her furs, clothes, a watch from Cartier and, of course, the 3½-karat engagement ring from Tiffany's.

Why, oh why, he asked himself, hadn't he gone through with the engagement and married her back then? Whatever had gotten into him to leave her and go off and marry Petra? The marriage had been such a disaster! In less than six months, Petra was gone and he was back begging Marie to come back to him.

My God, however could she have forgiven him? But that was Marie. She could always find it in her heart to forgive him. Or at least to admit that she could never stop loving him, no matter what he did.

About noon, as Jed strolled down 42nd Street back to the Grand Hyatt, he spotted Marie in front of him. His heart jumped.

Marie, now 24, was a woman people noticed. She was no longer the reed-thin, insecure kid in braces that Jed had first hired some years before. She walked now with the confidence of a woman who knows that the quick tattoo of her high heels on the pavement made men's heads turn. She had long, lean legs that made her appear taller than her five feet seven inches. Her wavy, light brown hair with blond touches hung down to her shoulders and framed a pretty face with large, hazel eyes and a flashing smile.

But Marie was more than a simple collection of attractive parts. There was something exotic in her eyes, something mischievous and mysterious.

She had on a black outfit that day—jacket, skirt, stockings, and high-heeled shoes, and a peach blouse, cinched with a large black belt. Gold earrings dangled from her delicate ears. She looked every bit the part of the successful young businesswoman she had become. She was an executive now, a woman on course. She shopped at Ann Taylor now, not Chuckles.

But her transition from a scared, thin kid into a confident, attractive woman hadn't been easy. For much of her growth had come because of—and in spite of—Jed Ardito.

Marie was born and grew up on Withers Street in Greenpoint, Brooklyn, a working-class neighborhood once solidly Polish and Italian. After years of resistance, its population mix had changed in recent years, as the new immigrants from the Caribbean began to fill up the apartments in the old row houses as previous generations of immigrants moved up and out. But the Danieles had occupied the same apartments on Withers Street for a half century, and were not about to relinquish their roots and move anywhere else. It was as if Greenpoint had grown up around them, and though it might change, they would not. Through thick and thin, the Daniele family had always stuck together, and they always would. It was an Old World tradition carried over from Sicily, and three generations in the U.S. had not changed it.

Marie didn't know it that Wednesday afternoon, not yet, but the tightly knit Daniele family was about to welcome two more new additions. Within two weeks, two of her sisters would discover they were pregnant. Marie would soon have two more nieces to play with and fawn over. Marie loved children, and looked forward to the day when she would have her own. But not with Jed Ardito.

Yes, it was spring; a time for new growth. And for Marie, that would mean new loves, new adventures. She wondered how things would turn out with Michael. She thought of what her friend Cara had said, about how good it would be for her to have a man treat her with some respect for a change.

Unlike Jed, Marie had no college degree. In her family, college was never really that important. But she was savvy enough to know how to make good money in New York. She was now making as much as $1,500 a week, and on her way to earning much more. For that, at least, she could be partly grateful to Jed. He had given her a break in the business when he'd hired her to work for him. But she had paid a price for all that.

She often reflected on all that he had put her through; these days, it was somehow less painful. In fact, she drew strength from recalling all the horrible things he had done to her, and all that she had gone through for him.

How she'd been forced to lie for him! When she and Jed began dating years ago, she'd had to conceal from her parents the fact that Jed was still married to his first wife, Heather. If they'd known, they would never have let him set foot in the house.

How she had to wait out his divorce. Jed said that he no longer loved Heather, but the divorce seemed to take forever. And all during that time, she had to look into her mother's and father's eyes and try not to let them know she was dating a married man. They had been so quick to like and accept him, to welcome him into the family.

Jed had been so loving and full of surprises in their first months of courtship. She would never forget July 20, 1990, her twenty-second birthday.

Marie didn't know it, but that date, July 20, had significance to Jed for another reason, too. On that very date five years before, in Bronxville, New York, on the grounds of Sarah Lawrence College, Jed Ardito had exchanged marriage vows with a young dancer named Heather

Hughes. But five years later, Jed was not celebrating a fifth anniversary. Instead, he now sought the hand of another. Even before his divorce from Heather was final.

He presented Marie with the huge ring, right in front of her parents, on the steps of Lincoln Center. Marie cried for joy—and perhaps also a bit from fear. Marriage was a very big step, and in the Daniele family it was permanent.

Marie's parents and relatives agreed she'd made a good catch. Jed was tall—six-foot-one. He was nicely built, handsome, and successful. He co-owned his own business. He had a degree from Sarah Lawrence College. And not only was he 100 percent Italian, but he was even Sicilian, just like the Danieles. And Jed seemed to come from a nice family. Jed's father had been a very successful businessman and was a Fordham graduate.

There was little said, of course, about Jed's mother, except that she had died some years earlier. It was only much later that the Danieles would find out the shocking, dark truth about Jed's mother. And, indeed, about Jed himself.

But the Daniele family welcomed Jed like a son. He had a place at the family table. He visited the other relatives. When it got very late after family gatherings, he'd sleep over in the Greenpoint apartment. He'd alternate with Marie's future brother-in-law, sleeping on the floor or on the sofa in the living room.

Marie was proud of him, and loved him, and loved him all the more for wanting to be part of the family. It was as if the Daniele family had been waiting for Jed all his life, filling out the parts that his own family had left so empty. For despite the outward appearances, Marie knew that Jed had gone though a most bizarre childhood, which had left him badly scarred and vulnerable. Indeed, that was one of the reasons she loved him.

* * *

During that first summer together, in 1990, Jed and Marie talked of their wedding date, and when they'd have kids, and how many, and what their names would be, and where they would live. They looked at their finances together, and drew up a budget. The weeks passed.

Then, suddenly, the world Marie was slowly and carefully planning, which was meant to last a lifetime, crashed into a million pieces. Jed suddenly broke off the engagement and walked out on Marie and her family. Just like that. For that blond Austrian stick! Petra, Petra, Petra. How Marie hated her!

Jed had met Petra Koss* swimming in the YMCA pool near Grand Central Station. He went for a walk with her afterwards, and boom! That was that. Within only weeks of his having left Marie, he was asking for the hand of this exotic, beautiful goddess.

It was hell for Marie having to work in the same office with Jed, seeing him, missing him, wanting him, while he only could think of Petra. Even his partner Eric talked glowingly about Petra all the time. Marie knew it had to be just infatuation. Petra was only a magazine cover, with no real soul, and Marie knew that Jed would quickly tire of her.

But he went off on a trip to Austria with her, where he met and charmed her parents, and formally asked Petra's father for permission to wed his daughter. It was the second proposal Jed had made within six months. This one did lead to the altar, however, in Austria.

Marie was crushed at the news that Jed and Petra would actually wed, only months after they had met. There was a big engagement party at Gianni's down at the South

*Not her real name

Street Seaport, and everyone in the office was there except Marie.

Petra, Petra, Petra.

All the men were wowed by her. Everyone agreed that Jed had landed a rare trophy. Petra was young, beautiful, educated, exotic, and wealthy. She was from a wealthy family, an excellent skier and horseback rider, and fluent in a half-dozen languages.

But Marie's intuition told her that she was just too good to be true, that for Jed she was more a fantasy than a real woman. Were such feelings only sour grapes? Perhaps, but Marie could not bring herself to believe that Jed, her Jed, could be satisfied with the likes of Petra. Not after what they had known.

And she was right.

Marie was later told the stories about the wedding outside Salzburg, a wedding straight out of a fairy tale. At the small country church in the Austrian Alps, Petra wore her mother's jeweled tiara. The celebrations included a dress ball, where all the men dressed like Mozart, with powdered wigs and false beauty marks, and waltzed the night away. Marie heard all about it. And each detail stabbed.

Just days after his wedding to Petra, Jed came creeping back into Marie's life, begging forgiveness, wallowing in despair.

This time there would be no long-drawn-out divorce. Jed quickly shed his new Austrian bride of only a few months.

He made promises to Marie again. He gave her jewelry. He took her on trips, trips which she was careful to conceal from her family, who now despised him.

Jed would later try to gain the good graces of her family. He gave a job to one of Marie's sisters. And he even showed up, late, at the bachelor party for Steve

Cairo, the fiancé of another of Marie's sisters. He was
not welcomed at the party, and was urged to leave. But
it would not be the last time Steve Cairo, a police sergeant
stationed in Queens, would see Jed Ardito.

Marie fell in love with Jed all over again. But how
could she ever trust him again?

2

As she rode up in the elevator together with Jed to the top floor of the Grand Hyatt, Marie felt confident, but at the same time also felt a twinge of fear. She knew Jed was not taking the change in their relationship easily. And she had seen what he could be like when he was angry. How could she ever forget?

It had only been a little over two months since that horrible night at his apartment on West 49th Street, when they'd argued, and he'd become so violent.

That night changed things forever between them. After that night, Marie needed no more proof that the sooner she got rid of Jed the better. He was getting out of control.

It was very early on the Monday morning of February 18, 1993, after a Sunday night of partying and drinking. Jed seldom drank much, but Marie, like a lot of women her age, would have occasionally have a few drinks while out with friends on weekends.

They argued that night. Lately, they had argued often. But then they would make up, and make love. But not this night. Jed was upset with her; he was losing control of her. Sometimes she would deliberately ignore him. And tease him. And even flirt with other guys, right in front of him. She was letting him know, in the time-honored fashion, that she just didn't buy his act any more.

They had a shouting match as they came into his building, and about 3 A.M. Marie burst out of Jed's apartment, intent on running out into the cold February night, even though she wore no coat or shoes.

Jed caught up with her in the lobby of the building, and tried to force her back upstairs to his apartment on the second floor. He grabbed her. She struggled. He persisted. She began screaming. Neighbors were awakened and came to their doors. A dog began barking.

"He's hurting me!" Marie yelled, as Jed put his hands around her throat. "Somebody help me!"

One first-floor tenant of the building, Michael Menard, could have behaved like a lot of Manhattanites who have been conditioned to ignore other people's problems. "Don't get involved" is a credo of survival in New York City.

But Menard could not simply roll over and ignore Marie's pleas for help. He got up from his bed, opened his apartment door, and saw Jed grab Marie around the neck with both hands. "Hey!" he yelled, in a menacing voice. "You better let her go!" Menard went back into his apartment and fetched a baseball bat.

Meanwhile, his girlfriend Lisa, frightened for Marie, picked up the phone and called 911. On the tape of that conversation, Marie Daniele's screams for help can clearly be heard in the background.

Jed tried to drag Marie back upstairs, while she continued yelling: "Help me! He's hurting me! Stop hurting me!"

Threatened with the baseball bat, and warned that the police were on the way, Jed let go of Marie and dashed off.

Marie then scurried into Menard's apartment. She was

shaking. She spoke to the police on the phone, and described what had happened. She thanked her rescuers, and said that she believed Jed would have killed her if they hadn't intervened.

By the time police arrived, Jed had fled the scene. They questioned Marie about the entire evening. She said that they had been out, that she had been drinking, and that she and Jed had a fight as they were coming into the building. She didn't want to stay with him, and had gone into his apartment to call her sister to come get her. But she hung up on her sister and fled the apartment because Jed was frightening her.

One of the policemen asked her if anything like this had ever happened before. "Yes," Marie said quietly, but added that this time Jed was angrier than she had ever seen him before, and she was afraid he would hurt her. The police then asked Marie if she wanted him arrested.

Marie fell silent for a moment. Like so many other women who are battered or threatened by their boyfriends or husbands, she hesitated. Did she really want to see Jed arrested? The realization that Jed could be so violent with her, could choke her with his bare, karate-trained hands, failed to register the way it should have. She should have thought of her own safety. She did not.

But instead of herself, Marie thought of Jed, and the trouble that he would be in if she preferred charges. "Do you want him arrested?" the policeman asked.

"No," she said. It was the probably the biggest mistake of her young life. If he'd been arrested that night, Jed Ardito might have realized that this relationship was over. Instead, he had reason to believe she was under his control, and that despite what she said she still loved him.

The police went up the Jed's apartment to talk to him anyway. There was no sign of him, but they'd had a report of an intruder in the back of the building and they concluded that was probably him.

A short time later, Marie's brother-in-law, Steve Cairo, a policeman then off-duty, arrived to pick her up. "What did he do to her?" he asked Menard.

Cairo knew Jed, and knew what he had already done to Marie and the Daniele family. Cairo had married into the Daniele family less than a year before, on June 9, 1992. He and his wife Antoinette used to double-date with Jed and Marie when they were all courting. He and Jed used to alternate sleeping on the floor or on the couch when they both stayed over at the Daniele apartment.

But after Jed broke off his engagement to Marie, got married, and then divorced, Cairo had no use for him. Jed still liked Cairo and had even thought that they remained good enough friends for him to crash Cairo's bachelor party in May of 1992. Jed was lucky he hadn't gotten his teeth kicked in.

Cairo thought that night in May 1992 would be the last time he ever saw or heard of Jed Ardito. But here Cairo was now, rescuing his sister-in-law from Jed. And it would not be the last time he would have to deal with the police because of what Jed did to Marie.

Cairo then drove Marie, still shaken, back to Greenpoint. Meanwhile, Jed had already reached safety somewhere else, the apartment of a friend, where the police would not find him. It seemed that Jed Ardito always had someone somewhere to turn to when he got into a jam. And so it would be on the evening of April 28, 1993.

As the elevator neared the top floor of the Grand Hyatt, Marie calmed herself. What did she have to be afraid of? This was broad daylight, no one was drinking, they both had a lot of work to do. What harm could there possibly be in having lunch and talking?

They went into room 3431 and Marie looked around approvingly. The room was large but it was dominated by the king-size bed. But this day, that bed barely would be disturbed.

Marie made some business calls. She also called her sister, as she did almost every day. Then Jed made some business calls.

Then they ordered lunch. He ordered a hamburger and fries, she a chicken sandwich with pesto sauce on Italian bread.

The food arrived about 12:45. When the room-service waiter came to the door, Marie concealed herself in the bathroom as Jed, his jacket and tie off, opened the door and let him in. Michael Byczek, then 37, had worked at the Grand Hyatt for years, and had learned to be quick and not to ask questions. Byczek set out the two food plates and a bottle of mineral water on the dining table, presented his check, was paid, and left.

The voice of Byczek thanking Jed for the tip would be the last one Marie Daniele would ever hear, other than that of Jed Ardito.

Jed had his little surprise for Marie—the pearl bracelet he had bought. She looked at it, but didn't leave it on. Marie had learned to be wary of Jed's gifts. There could be strings attached to them.

He had another surprise, too. A box of condoms. But that box of Ramses would never be opened.

Exactly what happened next only God and Jed Ardito can say for certain.

He would maintain that he and Marie made love, on the floor, and wound up engaging in rough sex.

Rough sex is, of course, the street name for sexual

asphyxia—a very dangerous practice in which one lover deliberately cuts off his or her partner's blood supply to the brain, by applying pressure to a major artery in the neck. The aim is to release that pressure just as the partner nears sexual climax, and the result is an intensified orgasm. "A Vesuvius of an orgasm," the district attorney would later say in derision. It's a risky way to heighten sex—and it can be fatal. If the blood supply is cut off too long, the individual first passes into unconsciousness, and then into eternity.

The practice is far from common, but men masturbating themselves account for the largest number of fatalities. In Westchester, New York, a few years ago, there was a spate of what appeared to be suicides—young men found dead with ropes around their necks. It was feared that another teenage suicide epidemic was occurring. But it turned out all the young men had been engaging in auto-erotic asphyxia—choking themselves to attain a better orgasm.

Some homosexual couples, say the experts, also engage in sexual asphyxia. But only rarely do heterosexuals play such a dangerous game. Did Jed Ardito and Marie Daniele practice rough sex that afternoon? Was her death just a tragic accident? Or did Ardito deliberately murder her by choking her to death? It would be a question a jury would have to decide. And on that decision would rest Jed Ardito's future—or lack of it.

Whatever happened, this much is clear. Sometime after lunch that day, Jed Ardito put his karate-trained right hand around the slender neck of Marie Daniele and squeezed the life out of her. For at least two long minutes, with his right thumb on the right side of her throat, and the other fingers on the left side, he squeezed hard enough to block the flow of blood to Marie's brain.

It took a minute before Marie passed into unconsciousness and went limp. But even then, Marie Daniele, young and healthy, could have bounced back if Jed had relaxed his viselike grip. But he didn't loosen his hold. He continued applying the pressure, even as she was comatose. He didn't let go, even as tiny blood vessels began to burst under her eyelids, inside her lips, and on the side of her pretty face. It was only after another full minute that Jed finally eased his grip, when Marie was already dead.

He stood over her motionless body, which could never respond to him again. Fluid began to run down her mouth. He carefully wiped it away, as if she were only sleeping. But she would never wake again, nor breathe, nor cry.

He tried CPR. Her lips were like rubber. Was this real or a dream? He tried CPR again, hoping for her breath to come back, for her eyes to flicker open once again, for life to return.

But it was no use. She was gone. And it began to sink in that with his own hand, he had extinguished the light of his life.

Looking down at the lifeless Marie, Jed could have felt panic, remorse, anger, grief, or, yes, even relief. But whatever emotions he felt, self-preservation was primary among them. The first thing he did was protect himself.

He did not call 911 or the hotel desk to report the death. He did not call a priest so Marie could get the last rites of the Catholic church. Instead, Jed Ardito picked up the phone and called a lawyer.

3

For someone who had never been in any trouble with the law, Jed Ardito's choice of an attorney was most unusual. He went right to the top—and his call was not ignored.

He contacted James LaRossa, one of the best criminal lawyers in New York. Indeed, in 1990 the New York Bar Association had voted LaRossa Criminal Law Practitioner of the Year. The bar association should know.

When lawyers get into trouble with the law, they hire LaRossa. When judges need top legal help, they turn to LaRossa. And when mobsters need the best defense that money can buy, LaRossa often gets the call.

Like most defense attorneys, LaRossa, who got his law degree in 1958 from Fordham Law School, paid his dues as a prosecutor before crossing the aisle. He was an Assistant U.S. Attorney for the Justice Department in the early 1960s.

But he has been no friend of the feds in recent decades. Among his more notorious clients was Big Paul Castellano, the former head of the Gambino crime family, who was gunned down in front of Spark's Restaurant on December 16, 1985, by a crew of John Gotti's goons. Indeed, LaRossa himself might very well have been gunned down right along with Big Paul and his bodyguard that night.

"Castellano had just come from LaRossa's office," recalled Joseph Coffey, then commanding officer of NYPD Organized Crime Homicide Task Force. Coffey knew Castellano well—he had helped build cases against him. In fact, it was Coffey who helped positively identify the body of Castellano at the morgue the evening he was shot; he knew Castellano's face well enough to do so. But Coffey also knew something else about Castellano that made identifying him twice as certain. Big Paul, who was in his seventies, had had a penile implant, the better to entertain his young mistress. When they picked up the body sheet at the city morgue, Coffey was sure of his ID. And he was sure of the guys who did it, too, although it would be years before John Gotti was finally brought to justice. Coffey not only knew who the men who killed Castellano were, he knew what kind of men they were.

"If LaRossa is in that car with Castellano outside Spark's, he's a dead man," said Coffey. "They wouldn't have hesitated to shoot him, too. He was fortunate not to have accepted the invitation to dinner."

But LaRossa's career was built on skill, not luck. His successes in court have brought him a lot of deep-pocketed clients, from organized crime figures to white-collar miscreants, including bankers caught up in the BCCI scandal. He has also earned a lot of enmity from some federal prosecutors—who don't like losing to him. In a backhanded tribute to his skill, the feds tried to prevent LaRossa from defending Wild Bill Cutolo, a flamboyant Brooklyn hotel owner charged with racketeering and murder. They charged that LaRossa was a "house counsel" to the notorious Columbo crime family, and should therefore not be allowed to defend Cutolo.

The attempt not only failed, but LaRossa fired back.

He accused the Federal Bureau of Investigation of protecting and abetting a known hitman named Gregory Scarpa, Jr., because he had turned informant. The FBI, LaRossa charged, had let Scarpa continue his deadly career as long as he kept on supplying them with information. Rare is the attorney who will take on the FBI, but that's the kind of lawyer LaRossa is.

So why would LaRossa accept a call and agree to see the likes of Jed Ardito, a struggling young businessman, who said he had just killed his girlfriend? And how did Ardito even know the name LaRossa in the first place?

For one thing, Jed had known LaRossa's two sons, Jimmy Jr. and Timmy, who had gone to Sarah Lawrence College with him. For a while after college, Jed and Timmy LaRossa shared an apartment in Manhattan. Jed had visited the LaRossa home. And there was another connection, too, one no one spoke about any more.

So James LaRossa made time to see Jed Ardito when he arrived at the offices of LaRossa, Mitchell & Ross at 41 Madison Avenue the afternoon of April 28.

LaRossa listened to what Jed had to say, gave him some counsel, and took care of a few things on Ardito's behalf—like telling the authorities that the lifeless body of Marie Daniele was growing cold in Room 3431 of the Grand Hyatt Hotel. Until LaRossa contacted the District Attorney's office with that news, no one but Jed Ardito knew that she was dead.

When the police got word that it was LaRossa who had reported a corpse in the Grand Hyatt Hotel, there was immediate speculation of a mob-related murder. Was the girl a sweetheart or relative of some wise guy? Or was the death related to organized crime in some other way? After all, LaRossa defended mobsters.

So a lot of police brass raced to Room 3431 of the Grand Hyatt Hotel after James LaRossa made his phone call. Meanwhile, Jed Ardito was in no hurry to turn himself in.

He knew that once the police arrived at the hotel room they would be quick to know a lot about the man who had been with Marie when she died. And they would also know some obvious places to look for him, since he had left his briefcase in the hotel room, and it was filled with everything from a copy of his birth certificate to his passport to a package of unopened condoms to his work calendar. There was even a photograph of him and Marie—with her face obliterated. There would be no mystery as to the identity and appearance of the man who had choked Marie Daniele to death that afternoon. The cops would surely be looking for him at his apartment and elsewhere. But Jed was not yet ready to surrender. So he headed for the apartment of a friend, where it would not be so easy for police to find him.

Denise Marshall was an important business contact for Jed Ardito, and had become, she thought, his good friend. They had been seeing a lot of one another in recent months, and Jed had often stayed at her apartment in Bay Ridge, where Denise, 35, lived with her sister. In fact, in the days leading up to the homicide, Ardito had practically been living with Denise—but not because of love or lust; he just needed a place to crash and a shoulder to cry on. Denise had known Ardito for six years, since he first began soliciting her for business. Denise, as a manager for the big law firm Mudge, Rose, was responsible for the hiring of lots of office temporaries—Jed's bread and butter. So he called on her often, and occasionally took her out for coffee, lunch, or cocktails. They were about the same age and became good friends, but not lovers. After Jed started dating Marie, the three of them would occasionally get together, and Denise got to know Marie well. So she, too, had a ringside seat from which to observe Jed and Marie's tortured four-year relationship.

Little did she suspect the role she herself would play at its tragic end.

During April 1993, Jed saw Denise almost every day, and often slept over at her Bay Ridge apartment. He was close enough to her that on April 27, the day before he strangled Marie, Jed went to Denise's office and told her he was going to take cash from her pocketbook—enough "to buy eyeglasses." In New York, a decent pair of eyeglasses costs about the same as a night in a good hotel like the Grand Hyatt—roughly $250.

Most of the time with Denise, Topic A was Marie. "He discussed the relationship often" she recalled. "She wanted to break up, and he didn't want it to happen."

Denise had watched the painful Jed-and-Marie show play on for years, and never believed they were right for one another. She even hatched a scheme that she thought would do all three of them some good. She wanted to back Jed in an office-temps business—but in California somewhere, far from Marie. Denise figured she could raise the money—$250,000 to $500,000 to get the operation off the ground—and she would take care of the business side. But Jed had not shown any great enthusiasm for the idea.

On the fateful morning of April 28, Jed spoke to Denise from his office. He needed some papers he'd left in her office the day before, when he stopped by to raid her pocketbook for "eyeglass" money. She faxed the papers to him.

But she didn't hear from him again all day, despite several attempts to reach him. It was nearly 7 P.M. when he finally returned her calls. "He called from around the corner," she recalled. A few minutes later, he turned up at her door and acted as if he'd had a typical day.

"We had a normal conversation," she said. Of course, about the time Jed was relaxing with Denise after his hard day at the office, police were poring over every inch of Room 3431 of the Grand Hyatt Hotel, trying to determine exactly what had happened to the pretty young woman who lay dead there.

But Jed did not spend a lot of time engaging in small talk with Denise. The first thing he did was to jump into the shower. Then he put on different clothes—he had left plenty of changes at Denise's in recent weeks—and took the clothes he'd been wearing to be cleaned.

Curious that a man who would later claim that his girlfriend died accidentally, in the course of rough sex, would be so anxious to take a shower and rush his clothes to the Laundromat. Even before he had spoken to the police. But not before he'd spoken to his lawyer.

In any case, no fibers or bloodstains or any other evidence from the crime scene would be found on Jed's body or on the clothes he wore on April 28.

Denise, suspecting nothing unusual—although Jed did ask her sister not to answer the phone while he was out—accompanied Jed to the Laundromat. Then they dropped by a liquor store and bought some wine. They also picked up a video to watch that evening. It was a typical nineties date, even if it was with someone who was only a friend: a little wine, a video, and home-delivered Chinese takeout. Except Jed Ardito had killed his girlfriend that day.

After returning to the apartment, Jed spent about an hour on the phone, Denise later recalled. One of the calls he made was to his boss, mentor, former partner and friend, Eric Goldstein. He needed help.

Goldstein will never forget the call he received at about 8 P.M. that night in his Westchester home.

"He told me Marie was dead," Goldstein recalled. "I was shocked."

Then Ardito asked Goldstein to call his attorney, James LaRossa. Goldstein called him and reality set in. This was no fantasy, no nightmare, and Jed needed a lot of help. But there was a limit to what Goldstein could, or would, do.

A few minutes later, Goldstein got another call from Ardito. "Jed kept on saying, 'It was an accident! It was an accident!' "

Goldstein remembered all the turmoil the couple had been through, and especially Jed's recent anguish over Marie's recent refusal to marry him. And now Marie lay dead. "I asked him if it was a gun or a knife," he recalled. " 'It was an accident,' was all Jed would say."

If Ardito was upset after making his phone calls, he managed to conceal it well from Denise Marshall for the rest of the evening. The only thing he said to her was that he was hungry.

She reheated some chicken parmigiana she had in the fridge, and ordered in Chinese food for herself and her sister. Jed wolfed down the chicken, and when the Chinese food arrived, he also ate some of the dumplings. After all, he'd put in a tough day.

What could be better to enjoy after dinner than a relaxing movie? About 10:30, with Marie now lying on a slab in the New York City morgue, and her family in despair at the news they'd just received, Jed Ardito calmly watched a movie. At no time did he tell Denise anything about the day's events.

"About 12:30 we went to bed," Denise remembered. And they slept soundly. "There were no sexual relations," she insisted. Indeed, she said there had never been any between them, despite the fact they shared the same bed on occasion.

4

Janice Culley is a big, blond woman in her late thirties who wears glasses and has a ready smile and a quick laugh. She looks more like a high school principal than a detective. But in 1993 she'd been on the job twelve years, five of them as a detective. On the evening of April 28, she was assigned to Midtown South, 357 West 35th Street, one of the more interesting and lively precincts in Manhattan.

You never knew what you were going to "catch" on a given night in that precinct—there was always a lively potpourri of crime going on, more than the usual stream of drug-related murders common in the city's other precincts.

About 6:30 P.M., while Jed Ardito was on his way to Denise Marshall's to shower, eat, and relax, Janice Culley "caught" the Ardito case, along with Detectives Val Troll and Al Regenhard. Sgt. Regenhard had just finished his normal tour of duty and changed into his street clothes when the call came in. It was well into the next day before he'd get any sleep.

It was not the kind of case detectives relish. Headache number one was the police brass, who began to gather at the crime scene shortly after the detectives arrived at

Room 3431, about 7 P.M. They'd all heard about LaRossa's call, suspected mob involvement, and had to come and see for themselves what was up. As Regenhard helped investigate the scene, he overheard one of the brass outside the hotel room ask a uniformed cop: "Who are those guys in there, dressed like that?" Regenhard remembered he'd been wearing his jeans and had chuckled to himself as he heard the policemen verify that the men in the room were indeed detectives assigned to the case.

Headache number two was the case itself. The perpetrator was still at large. He also seemed to have excellent legal connections, which would probably mean a trial. And in the course of the trial, Culley and the other detectives could expect that every single thing they did on the case would be very closely scrutinized by the defense. In effect, they, too, would wind up on trial. So they walked on eggshells, even more than they did normally.

It was highly unusual to come upon a crime scene so intact. Nothing had been touched by anyone. Usually, by the time detectives arrive at a crime scene, things have been disturbed. If there is a dead body, for example, uniformed police or others may have touched or moved the victim and other evidence to ascertain whether he or she was still alive.

"This scene was absolutely pristine," recalled Troll. "The hotel security guard opened up the door to the room for us. No one else had been in there since Ardito left."

They knew Jed's name from the hotel registration, and from LaRossa's phone call. Other police were at that moment looking for him. They did not know he was then taking a bracing shower in Denise Marshall's apartment.

The name Ardito clicked with Troll. In February, he recalled, he had been sent out to canvas an apartment building on West 49th Street, following a 911 report of an alleged assault by a man against a young woman, his girlfriend. The alleged assailant was Jed Ardito; his victim, Marie Daniele. Ardito had supposedly tried to choke her then; had he succeeded now?

Though there was no obvious evidence of any struggle, and no obvious trauma on the body, the detectives treated the scene like it was a homicide from the very beginning. As they went about their preliminary investigation, they sent for a crime scene unit, which would take photographs, dust for fingerprints, and go over the entire room with a fine tooth comb. The "A&S leather guys," as they were teasingly called for the department-store jackets they usually wear, were always busy. Based in the Bronx, crime scene detectives never have to wait for a call.

About this time, two other detectives were arriving at the Daniele household in Greenpoint, to inform the family of what had happened to Marie. They had with them a copy of the passport photograph of Ardito, fetched from the briefcase he had left in the hotel room.

Their dinner would grow cold that evening, as the family members collapsed in grief and rage. They knew right away who was responsible, and verified he was the man in the photo police showed them. Jed Ardito had haunted Marie's life for four years, and now he would haunt theirs forever. But by now, Jed was savoring his chicken parmigiana dinner, lovingly prepared for him by Denise Marshall in her apartment on the other side of Brooklyn.

Dr. Robin M. Rankow, the investigator from the medical examiner's office, arrived at Room 3431 at about 7:30. He carefully examined the body. Until then, despite their suspicions, the detectives had a "CUPPI case"—Case Undetermined Pending Police Investigation. But the medical investigator noted the finger marks on Marie's neck and remarked about them. It was about the only thing he said. Medical investigators don't say much at crime scenes, pending a full autopsy. But there was little doubt about what had happened here. She'd been choked.

Police brass kept on arriving at the scene. Over the course of the evening, a total of more than twenty police officers, from the chief of detectives to uniformed patrolmen, showed up. Some wandered into the hotel room, raising the possibility of contaminated evidence. At least that is what any good defense lawyer would claim in court—and of course that is exactly what happened later in the trial.

As Culley went about her work with the other detectives, she doubtless got some hard stares from some of the old vets on the force. There is still resentment against women in the New York City Police Department, and probably there always will be. It starts with the size and strength issue, and gets worse from there. Many male police officers don't like the idea of going into tough situations with women officers, and they will readily point to cases where women let their partners down because of fear, incompetence, or, yes, lack of physical strength.

These hard feelings toward women officers soften a bit in the detective ranks, but only on the surface. There is widespread belief that women detectives earn their gold shields more easily than men, so quotas can be met. A lot of male detectives refuse to believe that women detectives are as sharp as they are. It's a notion that is reinforced every time a woman detective makes a mistake. It's a notion that would be reinforced in the Ardito trial.

Janice Culley of course was aware of all this; indeed she had been living with it for twelve years on the force. But she knew something else about women detectives: that they brought a certain awareness and sensitivity to the job, an extra dimension that men lacked. Not just women's intuition, but insights and information that come from the experience of being a woman. And sometimes those antennae could make a big difference, especially when the case involved a female victim.

Photographs were taken of the room, its contents, and, of course, of the body of Marie Daniele. She no longer looked pretty; there was swelling and discoloration in her face, which would worsen as time passed.

Fingerprints were lifted off everything from the toilet seat to the glasstop table. Notebooks were filled with facts and observations. Sketches were made.

Culley looked at the victim, who was obviously just a few years out of her teens. She lay on her back, her headed tilted to the left side, clad in her bra, panties and a peach-colored blouse, which was open. Her black skirt, belt, jacket, and shoes were scattered a few feet away. And at her feet were the black panty hose, rolled up at the top.

Also on the floor near the body was a small white washcloth with bloodstains on it, and a green tablecloth, also bloodstained. Obviously, there was a strong suggestion that sex was part of this homicide. Condoms were in evidence, and the victim was half-clad.

Marie's body lay neatly stretched out on the floor between the bed and the table where she and Ardito had eaten lunch. The bed covering hardly had been disturbed. How curious. On a dresser top was an unopened box of condoms and a gift box and wrapping. On the floor, as if discarded casually, was the pearl bracelet Ardito had bought for Marie that morning. A single earring lay near the body. There was also a woman's portfolio and pocket-book. Within minutes, Culley knew for certain the name, address, age, place of work, and a lot more about the victim—including the fact that she liked jelly beans; there were a couple of packs of them in her portfolio. But perhaps the jelly beans weren't for her after all. Perhaps they were little gifts, the kinds of things aunts like to bring to their nieces and nephews. Indeed, Janice Culley would later learn that Marie had a niece whom she saw almost every day, and to whom she was very close, and often brought small gifts.

Jed Ardito's briefcase was also there on the floor, and contained a mother lode of information about him: copies of his birth and marriage certificates; his passport; a proposed budget for Jed and Marie, based on their incomes in 1990—when he first proposed to her; a lease on a new apartment—which he doubtless hoped Marie would share with him; credit reports—indicating he had been in deep financial difficulty.

There was also that strange photograph of Ardito and, apparently, Marie—with Marie's face missing. There were other papers, forms, addresses, and numbers.

There were a few things about the crime scene that bothered Janice Culley. One was the panty hose—they were rolled up at the top. That's not the way women usually take off their own panty hose. So they had apparently been rolled down by someone else, evidently Ardito. But she still had panties on. If they'd had sex, why would she have her panties on?

There was something else peculiar, too. There was no sign anywhere of any struggle. Almost nothing was disturbed—there were no broken glasses or upset furniture, no marks on the walls, nothing knocked to the floor, except the bracelet. That would indicate Marie didn't put up any fight.

But the way she lay so neatly positioned on the floor, between the unmussed bed and the dining table, looked suspicious. If they decided to make love on the floor—and why not use the bed?—it was a poor choice of floor space to pick. There was a lot more room elsewhere. And how could they have been making love and not knocked against the dining table? That surely would have disturbed some glasses, or the bottle of Perrier. Or at least they would have knocked the cart aside. It just didn't compute. If they decided to pass up the nice, big bed for a piece of floor, they picked a very odd place—between the table and the bed. Not much room to maneuver, without disturbing something. But the only thing disturbed on that table was a bottle of A.1. steak sauce.

Janice Culley couldn't help think that the whole thing had been staged; that things had been carefully rearranged after the homicide.

When her work at the crime scene was finally done a few hours later, Culley and the other detectives returned to the Midtown South Precinct and started to deal with the reams of paperwork that accompany any major case. Evidence had to be vouchered, forms filled out, reports filed. And in the middle of all this, she also had to contend with the relatives of the deceased.

It was well after midnight—while Jed Ardito slept soundly in Bay Ridge—that Steve Cairo, Marie's brother-in-law, arrived with two of Marie's brothers. They deferred to Cairo, who was a policeman.

The family filled Culley in on Ardito, and described the incident a few months earlier when he had choked Marie in the lobby of his apartment building.

So there was prior history of abuse—Ardito had actually attempted to choke Marie. And there was a police report and witnesses to prove it.

Cairo and the two Daniele brothers finally left the station house, taking with them some of Marie's personal effects—the last things the family would ever have of hers.

Steve Cairo would retain something else. The memory of going to the morgue over on First Avenue and having to positively identify his sister-in-law, from photographs taken of her body after death. It was Marie, all right, pretty Marie. But pretty no longer.

Janice Culley wanted very much to see and talk to Jed Ardito.

5

It was about 8:20 on the morning of April 29 when Denise Marshall set off for work from her apartment. Jed was still there—which was unusual. But Denise didn't think too much about it then.

She walked a few blocks to the subway, and along with a token she picked up a copy of the *Daily News* to read on the train. The *Daily News* and the *New York Post*, the city's two biggest tabloids, contain a lot less information than *The New York Times*, but they have distinct advantages over the broadsheet: they are a lot easier to fold and read on the subway, and they are a lot spicier. Many professional people read the tabs on the subway and then read the *Times* in the more spacious environs of their offices.

As she flipped through the *Daily News* that morning, choked as usual with gossip and celebrity and crime stories, Denise was shocked when she came to story about a murder in the Grand Hyatt Hotel the day before. With horror, she read of the killing of Marie Daniele. Police were looking for the suspect. Denise knew who that suspect was, and his whereabouts. He had spent the night in her bed and was now lounging around in her apartment, never having uttered a word to her about Marie's death.

Denise was still stunned when she arrived at her office, and she did not know quite what to do. Was she an unwitting accomplice to a crime? Was she harboring a criminal?

She called Eric Goldstein, Jed's boss and friend. Of course, Goldstein already knew that Jed had killed Marie. He said he would notify the police and tell them of Ardito's whereabouts, and she should stay where she was.

Later that morning police came to Denise's office and asked her permission to enter her home to apprehend Jed. She gave them a set of keys and off to Bay Ridge they went.

Until that morning, Denise Marshall had considered Jed Ardito one of her closest friends, a man she had known for six years. She had given a lot of business to him, and shared a lot of grief with him. She had comforted him often during many depressions, many brought on by his relationship with Marie. She had opened her home to him when he needed it. She had given business to his girlfriend Marie when, for about a year, he tried another line of work. She even offered to back him in his own business in California, giving him the opportunity for a fresh new start in a brand-new location, totally free of Marie and all the memories of her.

Yet in one day Jed Ardito had not only strangled Marie Daniele to death, he had also betrayed Denise Marshall. With Marie's body barely cold, he had casually come to Denise's home, changed and showered, without saying a single word about having snuffed out the life of the woman he was obsessed with.

Denise recalled how they had gone to the drop-off Laundromat, the liquor store, the video shop. She'd cooked him a meal, then they ate and watched a movie until 12:30 in the morning, and still he mentioned nothing of what had happened. How could he have done that? But Denise would have her day in court.

The *Daily News* was not the only newspaper to carry an account of the Grand Hyatt Murder. *The New York Times'* account a few days later contained some comments from James LaRossa, Ardito's lawyer. He called the killing "a terrible tragedy," and said that Ardito had come to his office at 4 P.M. that fateful Wednesday and that he then called the District Attorney's office.

"They were very close and intimate people," LaRossa is quoted. "They were sexually involved that day, and sex may have had something to do with it."

LaRossa thus firmly planted the seed that would become the mighty oak of Ardito's defense—accidental death, in the course of making love. The tabloids called it the "rough sex" defense.

The *Times* account also quoted Assistant District Attorney Harvey Rosen, who thought the killing did not appear to be accidental. He said that Marie had died after being strangled for three to five minutes.

Rosen also cited the "911" incident. "Mr. Ardito attacked and tried to strangle Ms. Daniele in February in the hallway outside his apartment. Neighbors heard the woman screaming, rescued her and called the police. Ms. Daniele refused to press charges." The legal battle lines were thus drawn.

Detectives Val Troll and Al Regenhard were among the hefty contingent of police officers who stormed into Denise Marshall's apartment. "We'd been told he was a karate guy," said Regenhard.

When the police burst in, Jed, in a dress shirt and his boxer shorts, ran across the hall, from room to room. "He acted surprised, but he must have known we'd be after him," said Regenhard. "But he was smug and arrogant."

Ardito clammed up when apprehended and read his rights. "He wouldn't say anything, to anyone," said Troll. "But when we got to the car, I had to find out something. 'Look,' I finally said, 'I know you don't want to talk to us, but you know the neighborhood: How the fuck do we get outta here?' "

About the same time as Ardito was puttering around in his shorts in Marshall's Bay Ridge apartment, Marie Daniele was under the knife of Assistant Medical Examiner Josette Montas at the New York County Morgue at 520 First Avenue in Manhattan. As usual, the medical examiner's office was doing a brisk business. Several other autopsies were being carried out at the same time on adjoining tables. The morgue could accommodate up to nine autopsies at the same time, and often did.

Occasionally, Dr. Charles S. Hirsch, Chief Medical Examiner for the city, would come by and inspect the proceedings.

Dr. Montas performed all the standard procedures, which are extensive. There are external and internal examinations of the cardiovascular system, the respiratory system, the gastrointestinal system, the endocrine system, the hematopoietic system (the spleen), the genitourinary system, the genitalia, and the musculoskeletal system. In addition, toxicology is done on samples of the blood, urine, brain, liver, and stomach contents. And finally, there is serology—often important in murder cases. It would be in this one as well. Samples of Marie's head hair, blood, swabs from the mouth, anus, vagina, nail clippings, pubic hair, and swabs from her right hand were sent to serology for analysis. An autopsy is the most thorough physical examination a human being can ever have done. And it's done when it's of no value to the patient.

There was ample, obvious evidence to indicate what

happened to Marie Daniele. "The face appears suffused with abundant petechiae [small hemorrhages] noted over the forehead, the upper eyelids, over both sides of the face, over the mandibular [lower jaw] area. . . ."

Petechiae are classic signs of blood having been cut off to the brain.

Further physical examination revealed how that blood supply had been cut off. "On the side of the neck is a cluster of three linear reddish brown abrasions of the skin. . . ." Marks from Ardito's fingers.

The report continued: "Symmetrically placed on the right side of the neck compared to the cluster of abrasions is a slightly visible . . . reddish-purple ecchymosis [bruise]." Ardito's thumb mark.

The official cause of death: Strangulation. The manner: Homicide.

The autopsy had revealed nothing unexpected; it was readily apparent she'd been strangled.

But there were some surprises when it came to the serology report. Despite the evidence of condoms, despite the fact that she was half naked when found, despite the fact that LaRossa had indicated sex had played a role in what transpired in room 3431 that day, no semen was found in Marie's vagina—nor in any other orifice. Indeed, no semen was found anywhere on Marie, or anywhere at the scene. Nor had any open or used condoms been found at the scene. The only condoms the police did find were still wrapped in their original packaging.

What about any female secretions? The autopsy report indicated only that there was a "very minimal amount of thick white mucus" found in Marie's vagina. That substance was not further identified. Thus the autopsy uncovered no positive evidence that any intercourse or oral or anal sex had taken place on Marie's final day on earth. And she was found wearing panties.

*   *   *

There would be no bail for Jed Ardito. Since he had failed
to turn himself in to authorities right away, he was deemed
a risk to flee. That was disappointing enough for him.
But he would soon be dealt an even more punishing blow:
James LaRossa would not handle his case.

6

Jed Ardito had no choice but to turn to his father for help with his case. He had no money himself, and no close friends willing to spend the seven-figures or so a top attorney would command.

So it was out of desperation that he turned to his father, a man who was practically a stranger to him.

Gerald Ardito, Sr., had never been close to any of his four children. As they were growing up, Gerald was seldom at home, rarely took the kids on any outings, or bothered with their sports or other activities. He liked to drink, and could get violent upon occasion. Jed did not harbor happy memories of his dad. When Jed got married for the first time, in 1985 to Heather Hughes, his father was not even invited to the wedding.

But Jed knew his father would do what he could for him now. For everyone who knew Gerald Ardito would know that his son Jed was in a very big jam. And Ardito Sr. could not afford to simply turn away his son at a time like this. That was not Gerald Ardito's style and never had been. When the whole world was looking, he had to appear to be a stand-up guy. It was his own reputation, not Jed's fate, that was at stake.

But Gerald Ardito no longer had the financial resources

he once had. He could no longer afford a top lawyer for Jed. And this was not a case which the district attorney was willing to plea-bargain—there certainly would be a trial.

So it fell to the court, and the taxpayers of the state of New York, to provide a lawyer for Jed. Here, Jed caught a break. Instead of some overworked hack who worked for the Legal Aid Society, Jed got an 18-B team. So-called 18-B lawyers are full-time criminal lawyers who sometimes take cases from the state, for a lot less than they usually charge.

Jed Ardito was assigned Franklyn Gould and Norman Reimer, partners in a highly respected criminal law firm. Even if he had the money, Jed could hardly have done better—shy of the likes of James LaRossa.

Gerald Ardito spoke to Jed's lawyers and learned that they needed to hire a private investigator. Gerald said he would hire one—for as long as he could afford to. Again, Jed Ardito got lucky.

Gerald Ardito put out the word that he was looking for a private investigator whose previous experience included a stint as a New York detective with murder case experience, someone who had been on the prosecution's side of the fence and knew what was important in murder cases—and who wasn't shy about getting information. The name Frank McDarby kept coming up, so Gerald decided to give him a call.

McDarby had been with the New York City Police Department seventeen years before starting his private investigation business in Queens in 1986. For most of those years, he had been a detective and had handled many homicide cases: stool pigeons shot and jammed in trunks of cars; deadbeats beheaded and stuffed into oil drums, then covered with wet cement and dumped in a creek; torsos of gang members who wronged their bosses and were found floating in New York Harbor, headless and handless.

As a coda to his career, McDarby had helped lock up the notorious Westies gang, a rogue group of thugs, junkies, extortionists, loan sharks, and murderers who terrorized and controlled the West Side of Manhattan from the late sixties till the mid-eighties. If he could manage that feat, Ardito thought, he'd be a great asset to his son's legal team.

The Westies were a throwback to the New York of a hundred years ago, when every neighborhood had its gangs, and most of them were Irish. They provided neighborhood residents with a source of protection against outside rival gangs, the government, and absolute poverty; in return they extracted protection money, ran the games and rackets, and siphoned off political graft.

But the Westies of the modern era gave nothing to the residents of the West Side, except a bad name. Their members were stone-cold killers.

The leader of the mob, who ensconced his own family in the bucolic suburbs of New Jersey across the Hudson River, was Jimmy Coonan. He and a few other of the gang members were Irish—fourth or fifth generation, but still Irish enough for the gang to be known as an Irish mob. This infuriated a lot of Irish cops. It bothered them that in an age when most Irish Americans had long scaled the wall into and beyond the middle class, there were still thugs like the Westies running around, stealing, doping, killing—and even doing dirty work for the mob.

In the eyes of many, their worst sin, however, was their total lack of charm or style. Instead, they behaved like mad, drugged rats, devouring their own kind. And they had very sick senses of humor.

One murder typified the gang's style and wit. Leader Jimmy Coonan was having a problem with one Rickey

Tassiello, who liked to make a bet now and then. Tassiello lost heavily, and borrowed a few thousand dollars from Coonan, who ran the local loan-sharking operation. Tassiello fell behind in his payments, but a relative bailed him out. But he bet and borrowed more, and fell behind in his payments yet again.

Coonan thought Tassiello deserved to be made an example of, so he took him up to a friend's apartment and shot him in the head. Then Coonan and his pals went to a local diner and had a hearty meal, before returning to the apartment to cut Tassiello into pieces. Most of his body parts wound up deep in the Hudson River, but Coonan got a brainstorm and saved his hands, putting them in a couple of Baggies and slipping them into his freezer. Coonan wanted to use the hands later to leave bogus fingerprints around at other murder scenes.

Another gang member killed a former friend of his, cut off his penis, and put it in a mayonnaise jar, which he then showed off in all the local bars. You never knew what you might see, or what might happen in the saloons owned or controlled by the Westies. Thawing hands one night, a jarred penis the next, a head in a paper bag the third.

McDarby had lots of reasons for wanting the Westies. They were merciless killers. They terrorized Hell's Kitchen. They had their mitts into everything they could—from the turnstiles at the U.S.S. *Intrepid* to the tills of restaurants and bars.

They also were users and traffickers in drugs—and McDarby hated drugs. When he was a kid growing up in Yorkville, a once working-class Manhattan neighborhood since gentrified into the Upper East Side, McDarby watched one of his brothers get hooked on heroin and die of an overdose.

The Westies also did contract hits for the mob. Anything

for a buck. They weren't poor immigrants fresh off the boat banding together to survive; they chose to be scum, and they disgraced and embarrassed all the Irish.

For McDarby, getting the Westies was an honor. It took the cooperation of several different law enforcement agencies, and a lot of persistence, but by the end of the eighties, the gang was no more. Most of its members wound up dead or behind bars for life. All, that is, except one: a man named Mickey Featherstone. And that bothered McDarby—a lot.

While a soft-spoken man not given easily to anger, at six-foot-four and over 225 pounds, McDarby engenders respect when he walks into a room. But in the early days of visiting the Westies in their favorite hangouts, McDarby was ignored. Briefly. The gang soon got to know McDarby very well, and came to appreciate that he didn't have to be angry to break your arm or loosen some teeth. With them, he liked to get physical.

"I had to," he explained. "It was like the old joke about the cowboy who needed a sledgehammer to saddle his horse. You have to get the horse's attention first."

Rousting gang members in their West Side haunts was McDarby's way of putting the gang on notice that the party was over, that he and his partners were determined to do whatever was necessary to nail them. And they did.

McDarby was just the kind of private investigator Gerald Ardito wanted—experienced, tough, and smart. But he had to turn on his considerable skills as a salesman to get McDarby interested.

A few days later, McDarby made it down to 233 Broadway to the offices of Franklyn Gould and Norman Reimer, the lawyers who were handling the Ardito case.

After talking things over with them, McDarby was persuaded that Ardito's story about killing the girl in the midst of rough sex was at least plausible for three reasons.

First, Jed Ardito had never denied he'd killed Marie. He called it an accident, but at least he didn't conjure up some story about a mystery assailant bursting into the hotel room and killing her.

Second, Jed and Marie had eaten lunch before the killing took place—immediately before. If he had lured her to a hotel room simply to kill her, it was unlikely he would have ordered, and then eaten, lunch beforehand.

Third, there was nothing disturbed in the hotel room. There had been no struggle—at least there were no overt signs of one. Yet there were indications that lovemaking had taken place. The girl was partially clad, condoms were in evidence, and the couple had been intimate for years.

But before McDarby agreed to work the case, he had to check out Ardito in person. Having been denied bail, he now awaited trial on Rikers Island, in the middle of the East River.

It had been nine years since McDarby had been to Rikers, but he remembered it clearly. No one forgets Rikers, not inmates, not visitors, not guards. Only God could forget the place, and he apparently did. It is America's Devil's Island, without the fun.

Old and overcrowded, Rikers is the temporary home of all manner of serious criminals who await trial or sentencing. A number of unlucky devils actually do serve short sentences there, although "short" is relative. Inmates have an expression: "One year in Rikers is worth two upstate." The correctional facilities which house permanent inmates, mostly located in upstate New York, at least offer jobs, education, recreation, and diversion. Rikers is essentially a holding pen from hell. Inmates have little else to do but look at the tantalizing city that is so near and yet so far, and seethe and scheme. Assaults are common, as are attempted breakouts (very few succeed, as the water is deep and the current swift). Sit-ins and strikes occur periodically. Occasionally, there is a suicide or murder.

McDarby recalled his last visit to the island. He was feeling very chipper that day, for he had the privilege of escorting Mickey Featherstone to the Queens booking center where he would be charged with the murder of Mickey Spillane, a fellow Westie. Featherstone was not the most notorious of the Westies—he didn't like to chop his victims to pieces—but he was certainly one of the most dangerous. McDarby and his boss, Joe Coffey, had long been accumulating information on Featherstone, and finally a murder indictment had come down. This, perhaps, would be the last of Featherstone. But he didn't seem at all rattled when McDarby told him what was up as they drove to the Queens booking center.

"Spillane? Naw, you ain't got it," he said. Featherstone was confident that was one murder rap he would beat.

As it turned out, Featherstone was right. He was acquitted of killing Mickey Spillane. But there was a lot more that he had to answer for. He later worked a deal with the federal investigators. If he would testify in the RICO trial against some twenty of his former pals, the feds would let Featherstone walk. And that is exactly what happened. Featherstone, a remorseless killer who admitted to four murders, five conspiracies to murder, and other sordid deeds, was rewarded for being a rat. He and his wife were put into the witness protection program in 1990 after he testified against his former pals, and all charges against him were dropped. It was the first time in his career that McDarby had ever seen anyone plea-bargain his way entirely out of murder. But the feds had a strange way of doing things. Indeed, the more McDarby was on the job, the more he was convinced that justice was, as he liked to call it, "a witch's brew," concocted mainly by judges and lawyers and ambitious prosecutors. It had little to do with good guys, bad guys, and victims. The worst sorts of criminals could often arrange the best deals because the feds were incapable of getting convictions without using rats.

A few years after the Featherstone case, the Justice Department would make an even more astounding pact with Sammy the Bull Gravano, confessed killer of roughly a score of men. He gave up John Gotti and other organized crime figures. So instead of spending the rest of his life in prison, he is also in the witness protection program somewhere, living off the taxpayers.

McDarby and a lot of other cops and detectives who had worked on the Featherstone case were infuriated with the deal that had been made, and they all lost some heart for the job after that. In fact, it was McDarby's last major case.

Bypassing the long, intimidating visitors' line where the relatives and friends of inmates waited to gain entrance, McDarby showed his ID to the guard and was led to one of the interview rooms and told to wait for Jed.

He wondered how the kid was making out. He caught himself—kid. Ardito was 34 years of age, over six feet tall, and in good shape. Nonetheless, McDarby knew that in Rikers, he was soft white meat in a black and Hispanic domain. He remembered an acquaintance of his who had done time there. Bob Bondini (not his real name) was a commodities salesman, pushing contracts for gold and silver which did not exist. It was beautiful for a while, and Bob lived well—an East Side co-op with a river view, a stable of girlfriends, a baby blue Mercedes convertible. But when investors who should have been way ahead of the game couldn't collect their money, the party was over. Bob was sent to Rikers while the local and federal authorities squabbled over who would nail him first. By the time the matter was settled, Bondini wound up spending two years on Rikers. He'd gone in thin and happy and come out musclebound and nasty. And he was lucky. Early on, he hooked up with a name mobster, a fellow Italian who put out the word. McDarby shuddered at what Jed might be going through.

So he was not at all prepared for what he saw when Jed was led into the other half of the room, behind the glass wall. He was wearing a full-length white robe, a black woolen cap, and sported a thick black beard. He'd gone Muslim.

"How are you making out?" McDarby asked.

"I'm doing okay," he said. "I'm learning to adjust. It helps that I know martial arts. I showed off some moves, and it helped. I have my father to thank for that. He made sure I got private karate lessons when I was a kid."

"How long have you been a Muslim?"

"Not long."

McDarby had reservations about Ardito's conversion. The seriously religious Muslims would be watching him like a hawk, suspicious of his convenient change of religion. If they thought he was faking it to better survive in prison, he'd pay for it.

On the other hand, all the other inmates might think he was a weakling. After only a few weeks in jail he conveniently wraps himself in the safe robes of the brothers.

But McDarby said nothing. He could see right away that Ardito was a survivor. After all, he was a salesman. The man had charm, humor, and he was convincing. He made you want to listen to him, and to believe him. So McDarby listened—but he didn't necessarily believe.

* * *

Over the next eighteen months, McDarby visited Ardito in jail at least a dozen times, more often than any relative or friend. He also visited saw Jed's sister, Dina, on his behalf, and spoke with Jed regularly on the phone. The men became friends—of a sort. The way a cop can become friendly with a bad guy. McDarby could never be 100 percent in Jed's corner; the only reason he knew him was because he had killed someone.

Jed liked to talk, and his favorite topic was himself. He was obsessed with his own life and history, and what had happened to him. It was as if his life were an ongoing movie in which he starred, but which was controlled by an unknown director. Jed acted out the scenes but wasn't really responsible for them. To be in Jed's world, you had to want to be in the audience, rooting for him. He managed to sell a lot of tickets to his own soap opera.

McDarby was cast as a producer of that same movie—his role being that of angel. It was up to McDarby to help minimize Ardito's jail term, so the movie could resume.

His specific mission was finding evidence to bolster Ardito's version of what happened on April 28, 1993, in the Grand Hyatt. Evidence of other trysts, for example, in other hotels. That would help support Ardito's contention that the date at the Grand Hyatt that day was not that unusual, that Jed and Marie had an intense, imaginative, and active physical relationship. According to Jed, they often went to hotels to make love.

McDarby also had to hunt for witnesses who could refute the prosecution's case. While there were no witnesses to the crime of April 28, there were several who saw what happened February 19, the so-called 911 incident. The prosecution wanted to bring up that incident during the trial, to demonstrate that Ardito had choked Marie at least once before.

7

Jed Ardito had a lot of time on his hands now; it would be many months before his trial came up. Lots of time to reflect on his own life, and that of his very unusual parents.

He had spent his earliest years growing up in Flushing, Queens, where he was born on January 23, 1959, in Flushing Hospital. He was the second child born to Gerald and Frances Victoria Ardito, the first son. His sister, Dina, was born two years earlier. He was named after his father and baptized Gerald Victor Ardito, but from the beginning he was called Jed.

Flushing was a pleasant working-class neighborhood. Bordering Nassau County to the east, it was almost the suburbs. But it was still the city, served by subway lines, permeated with the odd pride that New Yorkers have of living in "the City." You'll find a lot of very avid Mets fans in Flushing—Shea Stadium lies within its boundaries.

Most of the private houses in Flushing are simple, attached and semidetached homes, mainly simple red-brick structures containing two or three small bedrooms. Left to deteriorate, they could be as bleak as the council houses of a Liverpool slum.

But the people who live in these houses would never

allow that to happen. For most residents of Flushing, living there, and owning their own homes there, is the culmination of a life's work and dreams. The small front and back yards have patches of lawn as well-cared for as any golf course. The cheap, thin saplings which were once indifferently plunked along the sidewalks have been nurtured by residents into healthy, leafy maples. The wooden peaks and shutters of each home are often painted in different colors. The occupants have to make their homes distinctive and special, even though so many of them are so alike. Tipsy residents returning home at night have been known to knock on the wrong door.

But for a blue-collar worker in New York, Flushing represented a goal—it's about as good as living in New York City can get if you are a workingman; relatively low crime; not overbuilt with major apartment complexes, which private homeowners fight, since they don't want their neighborhood overrun with renters—people perceived as having no roots in the community.

Flushing has long had decent public schools, and good parochial ones, and is liberally sprinkled with churches. Like all Italian Americans, the Arditos were nominally Catholic. Like most Italian Americans, they treated the church like an old, dotty grandmother. Duty forced you to support her, and guilt forced you to be nice to her publicly (though ignored around the house). But you certainly didn't let her rule your life.

The kids would inherit this Christmas-and-Easter Catholicism. Jed was baptized at the Church of St. Andrew Avellino in Flushing on February 15, 1959. He went to Catholic grammar school and received his First Communion at St. Robert Bellarmine in Bayside. Nuns taught him his ABCs. But he was not religious—until, of course, his conversion of convenience at Rikers Island.

Growing up in that part of Queens afforded Jed plenty

of space. There were parks and open spaces where kids could play ball and ride their bikes and climb trees, and all within a subway ride of midtown Manhattan. On a clear day, from a tree in Flushing Meadow Park, or the rooftops of the taller apartment buildings, Jed could easily see the Empire State Building shimmering in the distance. Manhattan was close, but not too close.

Gazing toward the city, Jed Ardito must have dreamed of experiencing all the wonderful things Manhattan had to offer kids. Radio City Music Hall. The Museum of Natural History and the Hayden Planetarium. Central Park. Tickets to a live TV show. Little Italy. Chinatown. Putting nickels in the slots at the Automat.

But his father was always too busy to take him into town. Jed would have to wait until he grew up to enjoy the city. And by then, he was interested in other of its delights.

Unlike many of the other predominantly white, middle-class neighborhoods of the borough of Queens, Flushing was not predominantly Italian, like Howard Beach or Corona; or Irish, like Woodside; or Jewish, like Forest Hills. Ethnically, it was a mixed bag, the common denominator being a modest but solid family income. In recent decades, however, Asians have come to predominate; Flushing's Main Street now has more chopstick restaurants than pizza parlors or shamrock-bedecked pubs or bagel joints.

It was a pleasant place for Jed to grow up, but there were some horrible memories, too. They began early. When Jed was two years old, his mother gave birth to a boy who was christened Victor, which was also Jed's middle name—and a form of his mother's. Baby Victor would be the first tragedy to visit the Ardito household.

Jed was at an age when he was first becoming aware of things, when the first permanent remembrances are formed. These original etchings on a child's memory are usually happy moments—a birthday celebration, Christmas, a special gift from a special relative, the smell of a mother's perfume. Jed's earliest recollections would be of the freakish death of his baby brother.

Jed and his mother were out for a walk in a nearby park, the baby Victor was in his stroller. Somehow, the stroller tipped over—perhaps the wheel caught a rut. The baby spilled out and landed on the top of his head. As every parent knows, a baby's skull is soft on top, offering very little protection for the brain beneath. A sharp blow to a baby's head can be fatal. And so can a fall. Victor fell on just the wrong spot. He was dead a day later.

An acquaintance would later recall that after the death of Victor, "Vicki was never the same. That's when all her troubles began."

Jed was little more than a baby himself, but the trauma of losing his brother would not be lost on him either. As an older sibling, he was doubtless jealous of the attention a new baby always receives. Jed had probably wished Victor would just disappear once in a while. And then one day he did disappear, forever. Jed must have felt somehow responsible, as his mother surely did. It is impossible to be close to a baby who dies suddenly and freakishly and not feel some responsibility.

In 1966, the Ardito family moved into a house on Horace Harding Boulevard in Bayside, Queens.

For a view, the house provided a front-row seat of the Long Island Expressway, one of the most congested and despised commuter arteries in the country. It's a lifeline for commuters who live on Long Island and work in Manhattan. In the 1950s and 1960s the L.I.E. was the avenue of white flight for a generation of the city-born who wanted to move "out on the island" to raise their families. The apartments and row houses they left in Brooklyn and Queens and the Bronx were quickly filled by blacks, Hispanics, and Asians. And in their turn, some of these, too, would follow their white neighbors and coworkers out east to escape the city's crime and worsening schools. The L.I.E. was a pipeline of hope, but a nightmare to travel. Traffic snarls at two in the morning weren't unusual.

Day and night, traffic crawled along the L.I.E. outside the Ardito home. Sometimes cars would take to the service roads and neighborhood streets to skirt traffic jams. Cars were a constant in the Ardito home.

In the sixties, cars were as big and as powerful as they would ever get, before the days of the oil embargoes and skyrocketing fuel prices. Even garden-variety Chevvies and Fords had V-8 engines. Gas was 35 cents a gallon. Any kid with a steady job could afford a set of wheels with a 400-horsepower engine, and a pair of fuzzy dice. Drag racing became a national pastime, on tracks and along any suitable stretch of blacktop—like the service road of the L.I.E.

The revving of the engines, the blasting rock 'n' roll from the car radios, the yelling and cursing, the squealing of tires, and the occasional sick sound of metal ripping and crumpling all drove most area residents nuts—and they often complained to the police, who did what they could. But to Vicki Ardito's ears those sounds were like a symphony.

She'd grown up around cars, and now drag racing became her passion, her means of escaping a life that had become boring and tedious—and sometimes dangerous. She was 29, now the mother of three again after son Rickey was born in 1962. She felt trapped in her little house with the three kids. She didn't enjoy being a mother.

Gerald was seldom home, and when he was he often

reeked of Scotch and boiled with rage. Even the kids learned to avoid him when he came in, for fear of getting beaten. He had his own life, and Vicki intended to have her own too.

While he wasn't home often—and then rarely welcomed—Gerald did bring home the bacon. He was starting to make good money, and knew there would be more to come. He'd enjoyed a good measure of financial success in his life by creating a company that made boxes for perfume and other cosmetics. It was fitting that he should have made a career out of flashy packaging.

He'd gone to Fordham University, hardly a hothouse for entrepreneurs. In his day, graduating in 1953, with the Korean War now over, most Fordham grads became professionals—teachers, lawyers, priests, a few doctors. Or they thickened the ranks of banks, brokerage houses, and corporate offices as "executive trainees." These weren't for Ardito—professions where substantial financial rewards were usually a long time in coming, if ever.

Ardito, the son of a jeweler, was not one to wait. He preferred to be his own boss and take charge of his own fate. His niche became specialty packaging. At first, he worked out of his home, nurturing his little business throughout the 1960s, until he had his own block-square warehouse in Long Island City and a prestigious list of clients. The business became successful enough for him to enjoy an expensive lifestyle, which was the point of all the effort. Packaging was just a means to an end.

"He was a born salesman," recalled an acquaintance. "Good looking, self-assured. And a real type-A personality. He worked his ass off."

And he partied hard, too. "He was a 'Five Towns guy,'" said the acquaintance, referring to an area of Long Island called the Five Towns, hardly the stomping grounds for the elite. "He liked to chase skirts."

But he was not a man's man. It's one thing for a married man to cheat on his wife, it's quite another to make it a lifestyle. "He was a philanderer," recalled a school chum of Jed's. "And a sociopath."

Ardito paid a lot of attention to outside appearances. He dressed well. He drove big, new cars. His wife drove a Corvette. Eventually, he hired his own driver. His kids would arrive at school by chauffeur—not the best students by a longshot, but they made the best appearance. There was a full-time housekeeper. And when Ardito lifted a glass, which was often, his Scotch was Chivas Regal, never Dewar's.

He loved status, and all its symbols, and began setting his sights higher than a cookie-cutter house in Bayside, alongside the L.I.E.

As much as he hated the expressway outside their door, and the drone of cars, it was music to Vicki's ears. She loved cars for their speed, for the freedom they gave her, not any social status. With a drag strip right on her doorstep and her husband constantly at work or making his rounds, Vicki began street racing. It became the focus of her life, and she became very good at it. She'd take on anyone, and usually won. She thrilled at beating men at their own game. Drag racing didn't require size or brute strength, it called for guts, judgment, and coordination.

It also called for a good mechanic. Gerald acquiesced to Vicki's pleas and leased a Sinclair gas station for her. So she had a place to maintain her 1967 black Corvette, while also making a buck. She and her black 'vette soon became a legend at the National Speedway in neighboring Nassau County. She won scores of trophies, lots of prize money, and was recognized as the best drag racer in her stock class. She also attracted a slew of admirers.

Though she had given birth four times, Vicki kept her tight, lean shape and always took the time to do her hair and face right. She turned lots of heads at the track. She was a grease monkey's dream—a foxy broad who could really drive, who had a rich, indifferent old man, and even had her own gas station. She liked hot cars, and the men around them, and they liked her. At her gas station, or at her house, there was always a few young men bent over the hoods of their cars, one eye fixed on Vicki.

For Vicki, the summer was the best of times. School was out and the kids were shipped off to camp and she could indulge her passions without much distraction. The cloud of depression was gone. She felt alive and wanted and on top of the world. It wouldn't last.

8

Vicki Ardito must have been in her son Jed's thoughts. She haunted his childhood memories, and she haunted his present as he sat in his Muslim robes on Rikers Island, trying to figure out what in the name of God had happened to him.

How could the terrible irony escape him, that he had followed her example? Had she somehow planted some horrible time bomb deep inside him, one that was bound to go off when he, too, had to deal with rejection? Was Jed Ardito doomed to kill, because his mother was also a killer?

The press had dubbed it "The Motorcycle Mama Murder Case." It was the most talked about murder of the decade on Long Island. And it had become part of Jed's legacy.

The victim was Ben Mattana, a 28-year-old motorcycle dealer in Lynbrook, Long Island. His murderer was Vicki Ardito. On the night of April 27–28, 1976, Vicki paid young, reckless men to rob, kidnap, beat up, and kill the man who was her lover, the man she had left her children for.

It was Mattana's bad luck to start flirting with Vicki Ardito when she came into his motorcycle shop one day looking for new thrills, on and off the road. She wanted a new Harley-Davidson. And while she was at it, she also decided she wanted the man who sold it to her.

Mattana had no business fooling around with Vicki. She was sexy, with a nice shape and a funny, reckless way about her, but she spelled trouble from the start. She was ten years older than he was, married with children. Her husband was tolerant of Vicki's forays into the fast lane, as long as he could do his own prowling. But he was also a Sicilian, with a temper.

Mattana was also married, although not happily. But his marriage didn't bother him as much as his business. He was getting by, but in order to really thrive, he needed to move his Harley-Davidson dealership to a better location. Ben liked a good time, liked his drugs and women. All that took money. Mattana had no trouble getting all the sex he wanted. But he decided to take up with Vicki because she could provide something else besides sex— money.

But to Vicki, Mattana was salvation—the means to escape a life that had become more unbearable even as it became more comfortable. Vicki bet everything on Ben Mattana—her love, her future, her happiness. And she lost.

In the end, when there was no more money, Vicki Ardito would be told to get out of the home she had made for Ben Mattana. He said he didn't love her any more. He said he wanted younger women, and wanted to spend time with his young pals instead of sitting around with a nagging woman who was closing in on middle age, who no longer excited him. He told her to leave, and his ultimatum proved to be his own death sentence.

Vicki Ardito could not and would not leave Ben. So she hired assassins to snatch, rob, beat, and kill him, then dump him in a swamp. It took a month before police found his bullet-riddled, badly decomposed body in Howard Beach, Queens. The murder and its long, torturous aftermath left Jed with more than sad, horrible memories. His mother was capable of murder—his own funny, loving, though sometimes loony, mother was a killer. Would he kill too? Her lover had made her feel so hurt and angry and vengeful that she orchestrated his brutal slaying. Would Jed be driven over the same edge by someone who rejected him?

Like mother, like son?

9

The beginning of the end of the Ardito family dates from 1972, when Gerald Ardito was sitting on top of the world. His business was really beginning to pay off. He had plenty of money and the appetite to enjoy it. "He used to hit the clubs," recalls an acquaintance.

He had become bored with his middle-class home in middle-class Queens, and decided to decided to make his big move "out to the island." But not to any of the hundreds of tract housing developments that now stretched from New York City to the potato farms of Suffolk County. For a $1,000 down payment, young couples could get a three-bedroom home with a two-car garage, a thirty-year mortgage, and a four-hour nightmare of a commute back and forth from their jobs in the city each day.

That was not for Gerald Ardito. He bought instead in Old Westbury, Long Island. From the turn of the century, Old Westbury had been the province of Vanderbilts and Whitneys and the like, who lived in baronial manors surrounded by pools and gardens and acres of lawns dotted with fountains and statuary. Over the razor-sharp hedges were polo fields where men in crisp white linen pants and women in wide-brim hats took to the field between chukkers, sipping champagne as they tamped down the divots raised by the ponies' hooves.

Some of the great old estates were eventually broken up into much smaller parcels, which were affordable to the nouveau riche. The narrow, oak-canopied lanes and the split-rail fences and the patina of money remained. Even though the new inhabitants of Old Westbury were the hot stockbrokers and insurance salesmen and entrepreneurs of the day, not members of the 400.

The new, spacious Ardito home at 29 Meadow Road was barely a fifteen-minute drive from Flushing, yet it was a different world, and one to which the Arditos were ill-suited. They would not thrive here.

Jed was never a good student and his parents decided to send him and his younger brother and older sister to an experimental private academy in Kew Gardens, Queens. Its student body was overwhelmingly black. Some students were promising ghetto kids on scholarship; others the sons and daughters of successful black businesspeople; the rest were white kids whose liberal parents wanted them to grow up color-blind.

Vicki Ardito had herself grown up in an integrated neighborhood and always had black friends. She apparently believed her own kids would benefit from going to school with black students, too. Ironically, it would indeed help Jed much later, on Rikers Island. He knew how to get along.

Some of the kids were a lot tougher than those he used to scrap with in the schoolyards of the other schools he attended. He found himself losing fights, and vowed to get serious about self-defense. His father put some gym equipment in the Ardito home, which Jed used to build himself up. Later, he took up karate.

The Arditos had another child, a girl they named Toni. But the relationship between Gerald and Vicki only worsened. Jed didn't help. The old man was furious with him for being such a poor student when he himself had been such a good one. He was ashamed of Jed. Jed switched to East Williston Elementary School, which was filled with the promising issue of Old Westbury residents, but he did not do well.

Vicki Ardito, meanwhile, paid less and less attention to Jed's classroom difficulties. She had other things on her mind—chimpanzees. She'd taken it in her head to be an animal trainer. And once she got something in her head, she did it in a big way.

The first mail-order ape to reside in fashionable Old Westbury she named Tuff Guy. The kids were less than thrilled. It was difficult enough to get their mother's attention without having to compete with a wild ape running around the house. This was no cuddly little monkey from a TV cartoon show, but a scary, demanding animal who got more of their mother's time than the kids did.

Tuff Guy soon got his own sister and brother—Wise Guy and Tuff Girl. Breakfast at the Ardito household was literally like feeding time at the zoo—with three chimps and four kids running around trying to get fed. The apes had better boardinghouse reach.

Her idea was to put the chimps to work, making TV and movie appearances, showing up for mall openings, school events, and the like. Tuff Guy became a minor celebrity and even had a fan club. For Vicki, who always craved the spotlight, it was a bizarre way of getting into show business. She was only one step above following the elephants with a broom and shovel.

The kids learned to take a backseat to the chimps—literally. Vicki wasn't above some pretty lame publicity stunts to get work for the chimps. She wanted to make them stars—and big earners. Vicki had always wanted to have an independent income, and the chimps were her ticket.

She hired a public relations man to get exposure for her apes. One day she went to his office with one of the chimps and one of her kids, arriving in a chauffeured limo. After some publicity shots they decided to go to a restaurant in Bayside for lunch. But when they arrived, she didn't leave the chimp in the car, she left the kid. She made a grand entrance into the restaurant sporting a chimp on her arm. His table manners were what one would expect from a rambunctious two-year old—who was enormous, had great reflexes, an eclectic appetite, and no use for a knife and fork. The flowers on the table appeared just as tasty as the appetizers.

The chimp began to get out of control, so Vicki reached into her purse and pulled out a cattle prod, which she used to rein him in. Her child, meanwhile, sat in the backseat of the limo.

Her neighbors weren't amused. Besides the three chimps, caged in the Ardito's backyard, there was a menagerie of other animals, including several large dogs and a horse. They drew lots of attention to 29 Meadow Road, and lots of clucking from shocked neighbors. "She just wasn't the Old Westbury type," said one.

The animals weren't the only things that drove neighbors up the wall. Vicki had not lost her love of racing cars, and had recently also taken up motorcycles. There was always a fleet of assorted vehicles—expensive cars, dune buggies, minibikes, and motorcycles parked around the house. Old Westbury residents would sometime return home to find tire marks all over their showcase lawns, and they let Vicki know about it. Vicki, as usual, ignored them. "They should have 'Rest in Peace' written on their lawns," she cracked.

Along with the vehicles came crowds of noisy young

people, blasting rock 'n' roll, toking on joints, drinking beer, and tinkering with their cars and bikes. The police were called often to the house, something of a novelty in quiet Old Westbury. "If it wasn't for that family, the block could disappear and we wouldn't know it," said one police officer.

Vicki enjoyed shocking the neighbors with her friends and her tales of drag racing, using language described as "colorful." She dressed younger than her age, wore heavy makeup, large earrings, and lots of rings. "She was 40, trying to look 20," one neighbor told a *Newsday* reporter. "She was a swinger, with lots of boyfriends."

For the kids, home life was a circus. Vicki would encourage them to bring over their own friends, adding to the party. The Ardito kids became popular. Not many parents in that neck of the woods let their kids and their friends drink beer and smoke grass. Vicki let her kids party, but she ignored their other needs. She loved her kids, but also her chimps and her friends and her cars. And there just wasn't enough of her to go around. The lunacy at 29 Meadow Road continued as Jed attended Wheatley Heights High School, where he had a hard time. His bad study habits were hardly helped when he returned from school to a block party every day, and then a raging father at night.

Eventually, he was able to get away to attend a boarding school, Blair Academy. Why he picked Blair isn't clear. Perhaps there was a girl in the picture, for Jed had discovered sex, and was not unpopular with the girls. Nonetheless, Jed's father was thrilled; now perhaps his son would be able to learn something.

But Blair, too, was a bust for Jed and he came home again and returned to Wheatley. By this time, it was his mother, not only the chimps, who were out of control.

10

If television talk shows were around in the early seventies, Vicki Ardito could have been a serial guest on the Oprah–Donahue–Geraldo circuit. Some possible topics with which she would have been very much at home: "Women who run gas stations," "Mother of the apes," "Queen of the drag strip," "Obnoxious neighbors," "Older women, younger men." Lively, but pretty tame stuff compared to what she would have been able to talk about a few years later.

As she entered her late thirties, Vicki had reached a turning point in her life. She had managed to fill her days, and many nights, with a colorful set of diversions, but the bitter truth would always resurface: she was extremely unhappy with her husband and had a great need for love in her life. Her looks were fading. She had grown weary of maintaining the shabby facade of her marriage. And Old Westbury just didn't suit her.

There would be one more attempt at respectability, one more positive outlet for her intense energy and creativity. She opened a plant and antique shop in Huntington. She doubtless hoped that she could become financially independent enough to leave her husband and go her own way. But that was not to be. Instead of gaining freedom from a man who had become a stranger, she became more dependent than ever on a different sort of man who would be the ruination of her life.

Benjamin Mattana was a young man with ambition. Not yet out of his twenties, he owned a Harley-Davidson franchise on 289 Merrick Road, in Lynbrook, Long Island, and wanted to move it to a better location. He took plenty of time to sniff the daisies, in the pre-AIDS era when sex, drugs, and rock 'n' roll were the mantra for a generation fed up with the Vietnam War. But Ben kept his focus. He was going to do well in his world, despite the fact that he had no college education or easy access to capital. It was ironic that, like Vicki's husband Gerald, he was Sicilian and had the same sort of drive—except that he would treat Vicki even worse than Gerald had.

It was her interest in motorcycles that brought her into the selfish, scheming world of Ben Mattana. She drove a Harley; he sold and serviced them. But he wasn't the first guy with grease under his fingernails to whom she took a fancy.

When she ran the Sinclair station in Queens, she took a young man named John Dellacona under her wing. He was just a teenager then, from Brooklyn, in love with cars and racing and speed and Vicki Ardito. She liked the kid, and he became a regular at the station and in the Ardito home. She became his surrogate mother—as if her own four kids, the menagerie of pets, and the trio of apes were not enough to satisfy her motherly instincts.

Another frequent visitor to 29 Meadow Road was Sebastian (Benny) Ventimiglia, a sometime mechanic from South Ozone Park, in Queens. He came from a rough neighborhood, but Bennie could more than hold his own. He was 20, tough, and a karate expert. He spent some of his time at the Ardito home instructing young

Jed in the martial arts, and he was a very good teacher. Jed might have had trouble learning in the classroom, but he took to karate quickly. And he would not forget what he learned.

Ben Mattana's relationship with Vicki Ardito would never have lasted as long as it did, nor ended as savagely, if it weren't for two things—Vicki had access to money, and she was deeply in love with him. The fatal element was that she would not be easily dismissed when she didn't get what she wanted.

In the fall of 1974, right around the holiday season, Vicki moved out of the splendid Old Westbury home and took up residence with Mattana in his modest house which he was trying to fix up, at 107 Browns Road, in Lloyd Harbor. There was much to be done—the home had originally been a chicken coop.

She soon applied her artistic talents to fixing up the place. But there was only so much curtains and a woman's touch could do without some major renovation, and Vicki soon started putting money into the house, money she received from her estranged husband.

She was receiving $540 per month from Gerald as part of their separation agreement; much of this went into fixing up the Mattana home, but it wasn't enough. And Mattana also needed more money, to move his motorcycle dealership. He pressured Vicki to get some cash out of her husband. She had an interest in the Old Westbury house, and could use that as leverage to get a lump sum from Ardito. She negotiated as best she could, and as soon as any money arrived she handed it over to Mattana. She loaned him at least $19,000 in one shot. Some of it went into the house, some of it was earmarked for the business, and some of it doubtless went to drugs and partying.

But the young Mattana began to tire of this woman

who was ten years his senior and had begun to take over his life. He wanted other women. He wanted to pal around more with friends instead of sitting home with Vicki, who made his meals, kept his house, and encouraged him in his business. She ran her shop, and still managed to see her children at the Old Westbury estate almost every day. They now ranged in age from three to seventeen and, with their father absent so often, still very much loved and needed their mother.

After she loaned him the $19,000, Mattana's interest in Vicki began to diminish. Gerald was not about to simply hand over any more money to a woman who had walked out on him for a younger man, regardless of how empty their marriage had been. The divorce would take a while, and Gerald would fight to keep as much as he could out of Vicki's—and Mattana's—hands.

Ardito hired a private detective to help make his case against Vicki in the divorce proceedings. The dossiers filled fast.

Finally, after about eighteen months of living together, and with Vicki now broke, Mattana put it to Vicki bluntly:

"I want you out."

Adding insult to injury, he had also told her that he had no intention of paying her back any of the money she had loaned him, or to pay her anything for all that she had contributed to their home and its upkeep during the time they were together. He wanted to get rid of Vicki as quickly and painlessly as possible, and made his wishes clear.

Vicki was devastated. She still adored Mattana, and had sacrificed all she could for him. But her young handsome lover knew what he wanted—and it wasn't Vicki.

For months Vicki pleaded with him, but he only became more insistent that she pack up and go immediately. He wanted her out of his life permanently.

Vicki was getting despondent, and began hatching wild schemes. She couldn't and wouldn't move out on the man she loved so much. She couldn't wheedle any more money out of her husband. At least not legally.

Just how desperate she had became would not surface until later, but in the fall of 1975 Vicki actually plotted to kidnap her own daughter, four-year-old Toni. The plan called for a $50,000 ransom, which she knew her husband could afford. Mattana apparently had no objections to the scheme—as long as he would get his hands on the proceeds.

The plan never came to fruition, as Vicki entered into negotiations with her husband to get a lump-sum payment in exchange for her half-interest in the Arditos' Old Westbury house, then valued at about $250,000, but negotiations dragged on.

"She didn't have a dime," said John McCarthy, an FBI agent who later was assigned to the Mattana case and uncovered the scheme to kidnap the daughter. "She had to give all her money to Mattana." The money from the kidnapping was to have been used to move Mattana's motorcycle dealership from Lynbrook.

But a dark seed had been planted in Vicki's head—the idea of a kidnapping. She had always been a gutsy woman, and did things few other women or men would dare. Indeed, to her long list of dubious achievements would soon be added kidnapping. Her own daughter would not be the victim, but someone else very dear to her would be.

By the spring of 1976, Vicki Ardito was at the end of her rope. Her lover was picking fights with her, telling her to get out. And he still refused to pay her back a dime.

On April 24, Vicki confided her desperation to two

employees who worked at her plant and antique shop, called Vicki's Plantique, in Huntington.

"She said there was something she wanted to tell us, but she didn't think she could trust us," said Jamie Kurzweil. "She was afraid we wouldn't believe her. I think she wanted us to drag it out of her."

Finally, Vicki blurted it out. "She said she couldn't stand it any more," recalled Kurzweil. "She was going to kill Ben."

Kurzweil knew that the two had not been getting along. She said that when she first started working in the shop, in December of 1975, Ardito and Mattana "got along beautifully." But by the end of March, there was a big change. "They were constantly haggling," she said. "Ben would go out of his way to hurt Vicki mentally, to cause her mental anguish."

Kurzweil knew Vicki was unhappy, but couldn't take the threat seriously. "I took it as someone being mad and saying, 'I'm going to kill you,'" she said. "I thought it was out of anger."

She knew Vicki's plight. "She didn't want to leave Ben. She had nowhere to go. She couldn't go back to her husband. My mother and I offered to have her stay with us."

And Kurzweil knew that Vicki had reason to think violently. After Vicki had failed to raise more money for him from her estranged husband, Mattana had "smashed the house up."

Still, Kurzweil couldn't imagine that her boss would actually carry out the murder threat. Jamie was not the first nor the last person to underestimate Vicki.

11

Vicki Ardito fantasized about ways to kill Mattana. A witness would later testify that she hatched at least three plots. The first could be chalked off as the sort of scheme that any rejected lover might concoct—neat in the mind's eye, poetic in a way, but almost impossible to execute. She wanted to ride him on his motorcycle off a cliff into Long Island Sound. It was preposterous.

The other schemes were not so outrageous. She talked of substituting pure cocaine for the "stepped-on" drug he was using, so he would die of an overdose; or of giving him a fatal injection of insulin.

Vicki abandoned those schemes, not because they weren't feasible, but because they simply wouldn't punish Mattana enough. She wanted him to suffer for what he did to her, and ultimately he did.

She would need accomplices to the diabolical plan she eventually hit upon. She needed someone who was tough, and she needed someone she could trust.

Benny Ventimiglia was a logical choice, the out-of-work mechanic who hung around the Ardito home in Old Westbury and was giving karate lessons to Jed. He was fearless, he needed money, and he was not one to turn down a challenge to his manhood.

In addition, she needed someone she could rely on. She thought of 24-year-old John Dellacona to help her. He was a technician at Creedmore State Hospital, a mental institution in Queens. He had known Vicki for about ten years, ever since his father had turned over the Sinclair gas station to her. He continued to hang around the gas station, running errands and puttering with cars. Vicki became a sort of surrogate mother to the then-15-year-old Brooklynite, and they remained close for years. "There were times when Vicki supplied me with cocaine," he later testified. He also testified that Vicki had made him an extravagant promise if he would go along with her plan. "She said to me, " 'If you help me get rid of Ben you won't have a thing to worry about for the rest of your life.'" He ultimately did participate, but only after being coerced.

A third man—just a kid, really—was also brought into the plot, 16-year-old Mario Russo, a big but baby-faced Brooklyn kid who worked as a counterman in his father's pizzeria. He was a late entry.

A picture of Vicki Ardito's state of mind in the spring of 1976 sadly emerged later at the trial when a tape recording was played for the jury. She would often leave taped messages for Mattana. He was not the sort of man who would sit still and quietly listen to what was on her mind, so she would leave taped messages for him. Like mother, like son.

One evening, while he was out getting some cooking oil she needed to prepare dinner, she poured out her thoughts. They were confused. She rambled. But the tapes were a last, desperate cry for help.

She avowed her undying love for him. "You have to say to yourself, 'Ben, would I actually do this—give up my life for Vicki?' I don't think so, Ben. But I know I would. . . . "

She alluded to the little, specific events that showed Mattana's lack of love for her. "I know you don't want me here anymore. You made that pretty obvious.

"You came home at 8:30. You didn't say anything. You went out with your brother instead of with me. You came home tonight and it was pick on Vicki! Vicki did everything wrong."

She said how much she appreciated their time together, though it was infrequent.

"But you know what, Ben? All I ever wanted was just to be alone with you. Whether we were watching television or sitting at the kitchen table, that's all I've ever wanted. And we haven't been alone. It's always people around. Remember how nice we used to get along when we were alone? It's always people interfering with our lives."

Her voice cracking, she went on like a lovesick teenager. "Oh, Ben, you never used to be like this. You took care of me. You carried me around on a pedestal. You were so proud to take me with you. Anywhere you went, Vicki went."

The state of her desperation was clear as she went on, and if Mattana listened to the tape at all, he might have gotten a clue as to just how distraught and dangerous Vicki was. "Please don't make me go back. Please, I beg of you. I beg you in front of the entire world. Stop me, Ben, please . . . show me that you care. Please help me. I'm so very lonely. Help me. Don't make me think of you this way. Let me think of you the way I thought of you before. Please be different when you walk in. . . . "

Vicki's whining fell on deaf ears. Mattana was more determined than ever to get rid of Vicki. Who needed her anymore? She had failed to get any more money out of her husband, she was interfering with his love life with other women and with his desire to party. She was a homebody in her late thirties and past her prime. He was not yet thirty, and there were a lot of women he could share his bed with who were younger, better looking, and didn't nag him. There was one girl in particular he was seeing a lot of. Who needed this grief? Vicki's pathetic, tape-recorded messages not only left Mattana unmoved, they intensified his resolve to dump her.

There was no question Vicki Ardito was becoming unhinged, but she still managed to mastermind a vicious contract killing, and to see that it was carried it out. But Vicki gave little thought to what would happen after the fact. She conceivably could have gotten away with doing in Mattana by giving him a cocaine overdose or even an insulin injection, but the complications of her ultimate scheme, and inevitable wide trail left behind by her accomplices, practically assured that Vicki Ardito would not get away with it. At the time, it didn't seem as if she cared very much whether she did or not. She just wanted vengeance.

12

On April 27, 1976, Vicki Ardito put into action her plan for the kidnapping, robbing, and killing of Mattana.

Her scheme involved staging a kidnapping—armed men abducting Mattana from his home at gunpoint, while Vicki looked on. Ben would disappear, and she would have her alibi. She would claim that she, too, was threatened by the gunmen, but had no part in what had happened to Mattana.

The plan further called for the abductors to take Mattana to his store, so they could rob whatever was in the safe. That would make it appear the motive of kidnapping Mattana was to rob him, and the assailants could be almost anyone who knew that he always had cash in his safe.

Ideally, Ben Mattana would then disappear off the face of the earth and no one, save his killers, would know what happened to him. Vicki didn't care, as long as he was beaten up first and permanently disposed of. Wronged by the man she loved, she insisted that he suffer for what he did to her and never breathe another day.

Her accomplices, Benny Ventimiglia and Mario Russo,

were to be paid $10,000 each, plus whatever they robbed from Mattana's cycle shop.

Vicki's plan was not as well thought out as it might have been. Important details were ignored. One involved a dog, a snarling German shepherd, Mattana's watchdog. Because the dog might interfere with the kidnapping, Vicki wanted him out of the way. So in the late afternoon of April 27, before Mattana came home, Vicki turned to a next-door neighbor and asked a favor.

Described as a nice neighborhood kid, James Pape, 18 was friendly with Mattana and Vicki and would occasionally run errands for them.

"Would you be a doll and run Ben's dog down to my shop in Huntington?" she asked him. Pape said he'd be happy to oblige.

But when Pape arrived at Vicki's Plantique, Ardito's assistant in the store, Jamie Kurzweil, hit the roof. "He'll wreck the place!" she said, sending Pape back to the house in Lloyd Harbor. Vicki had failed to alert her assistant to take the dog off her hands for a while—or to give her a reason why. It would prove to be a major oversight.

Pape returned the German shepherd to the house in Lloyd Harbor—and promptly ran into a scrape with death.

The men Vicki had hired were already at the house, waiting for Mattana to come home. Instead, Pape walked in with the dog. He saw the men handling a gun.

"What the hell is going on, Vicki?" Pape asked her.

"Nothing," she replied. She didn't want him involved. But the men had a problem. Pape had seen them in the house and with a gun. He might be able to identify them later. But the plan was complicated enough without adding on another killing, and time was running short. Ventimiglia instead threatened Pape with death if he talked to anyone about the gun. Terrified, Pape fled the house and returned next door.

Vicki then took the dog to a storeroom in the back of the house, where he would be out of the way and not be able to interfere with the kidnapping. All was in readiness.

Not long afterward, Ben Mattana approached his house in Lloyd Harbor half-dreading going inside. Vicki just wasn't getting the message and had been such a whiner lately that he couldn't stand being around her. Christ, couldn't she just go home to her kids? Her old man would take her back—for a while at least. He could afford it, the bastard. He was a millionaire, and he didn't even have to break a sweat. Well, maybe once he got the new motorcycle shop he'd be on his way. Without that nag Vicki.

Accompanying Mattana was a friend—it was Tuesday night, and that was the night he went over to the friend's house to watch wrestling on television. Vicki had not thought of the possibility that Ben might not come home alone. The killers had another problem on their hands.

When the pair walked into the house Vicki seemed a little nervous—but she always seemed nervous these days. Mattana said nothing and went to get a beer. "I'm going to the wrestling tonight," he said. "You're going too."

"Aw, Ben. Let's skip it tonight. Let's stay home," she said, fearful that the delay could wreck her plan. The gunmen were lurking in a rear bedroom, listening through the door. They had been all set to pounce on Mattana had he not had a friend with him. Vicki wanted the friend to leave and for Ben to stay home. But it was no dice. It was the last thing he ever refused her. Had he obliged he only would have died sooner.

"We're going to watch the wrestling matches," he insisted. "Get your shit."

Before she left, Vicki managed to slip into the bedroom where the would-be killers were hiding, and she told them to sit tight. "We'll do it after we come back," she said. "I'll call you here and keep you posted on the time."

There had already been two disruptions to Vicki's plan, and more experienced criminals might have aborted things right there. Things were not going well. But they decided to go ahead, anyway, and after Vicki and Mattana left with Ben's friend to watch the wrestling matches, they sat down and awaited Mattana's return.

For Benny Ventimiglia, the delay was merely an annoyance. He had committed armed robbery before, and wasn't going to get a nervous stomach over this.

Mario Russo must have found the wait tougher to handle. He really didn't know anyone involved, and had only spoken to Vicki over the telephone, when she called him at his father's pizza parlor. He was only sixteen, and had no criminal record.

John Dellacona, Vicki's friend, was also apprehensive. He had refused to play any role in the murder, but had been forced by the others to be their driver.

The hours dragged on. Finally, the phone rang. There was no telling exactly who might be on the line, but Vicki had said she would call and they agreed to answer the phone.

From her end, Vicki, who was in Ben's friend's house nearby, pretended to be using the phone to check that the kid next door, James Pape, had come over to feed the dog, as she'd asked him to do. Pape, of course, was sitting in his own house, terrified, wondering what might be going on next door. But he feared too much for his life to tell anyone that he had seen men with a gun lurking in Mattana's house.

After talking briefly with Vicki, Ventimiglia assured the others that everything was still on, and they got ready for Mattana's return. Then he did something which no professional killer would dream of. He picked up the phone and called his girlfriend, Annamarie Pugliese, 21, of South Ozone Park, Queens. Pugliese had been dating Ventimiglia, and spent a lot of time at his home. She knew he was often involved in criminal activity. Just the previous evening, he had warned her that if police should come looking for him, she should say that he had gone to Philadelphia.

Sometime afterward, they heard a car door slam. Finally, it was time to get on with it.

13

When Mattana came into the house with Vicki, he was surprised by the three men. He was no match for the karate-skilled Ventimiglia, who promptly carried out Vicki's first wish and pistol-whipped him.

If Vicki then had any second thoughts over her plan, as she watched the man she loved so much being humiliated and beaten with a gun, she kept them to herself. But Mattana had no idea that it was her scheme that was being played out. He thought he was going to be robbed, and that would be the end of it.

"We're going to your shop in Lynbrook," he was told. "You have money in the safe there, right? You'd better."

Since Vicki had told her hired assassins they could keep what was in the safe, that was then their first concern. The $10,000 which she had promised them would have to come later—after she got money from her husband as part of the divorce settlement, or after Mattana's house was sold. Vicki had a lien on the house for the $19,000 she had loaned Mattana. But at that time, she was broke.

Ventimiglia especially had need of that money in the safe—he was in debt to a cocaine dealer. Not only was it dangerous to owe a drug dealer money, it also cut off your supply. Vicki had told the men that Mattana often kept as much as $8,000 in the shop.

Bleeding from the pistol-whipping, Mattana was asked for the combination to the safe in his Lynbrook shop. Russo jotted the numbers down on whatever was handy—which turned out to be Vicki Ardito's registration for the Kawasaki motorcycle.

But Mattana didn't have the keys to enter the shop. They were in the possession of his store manager, who lived in nearby Uniondale.

Accounts differ as to exactly what happened next—whether Mattana was taken in Vicki's rented car to the manager's home, or whether it was Vicki who went while Mattana was held at gunpoint in his house.

The store manager delivered the keys, either to Mattana or Vicki, and the robbers proceeded to the motorcycle shop.

When they finally gained entrance to the shop and opened the safe, the robbers were not amused. There was only $1,200 in the safe, a lot less than what they expected.

They were in a sour mood as they turned to the final phase of the evening's dirty work. They returned to Mattana's house, and the three men proceeded to take Ben Mattana on the last ride of his life. Vicki stayed behind.

Having grown up in South Ozone Park, Benny Ventimiglia knew the nearby marshes of Howard Beach well. Divided by Cross Bay Boulevard, the marshland is part bird sanctuary, part makeshift dumping ground. At this time of year, late April, the seven-foot-tall reeds of the previous season's salt hay are stiff, and the bristles on their ends bushy. In a few weeks, new shoots would start to displace them. But only a few yards from the road, the deserted marshes were a good place to hide. Birds knew that, and so did Ventimiglia. On pleasant nights, he even used to take his girlfriend Annamarie there.

It's about an hour's drive from Lynbrook to Howard Beach, and by now Ben Mattana had to be fearing the worst. If they were going to let him go, they would already have done so.

Mattana kept on trying to see if there were any cars following them. Surely, Vicki must have alerted the police by now. They must be looking for them. They would have the make and the license plate of the car. And it was late at night, without much traffic. The car should be a cinch to spot.

But as they drove on, there would be no police chasing them or even looking for them. Vicki Ardito had not called anyone at all, of course. And the thought finally had to come to Ben Mattana that Vicki was in on it. Christ, the bitch had orchestrated the whole thing!

When they finally pulled up in a deserted spot, Russo and Ventimiglia dragged him out of the car and deep into the marsh. Dellacona waited nervously in the car.

All was quiet. The men were out of earshot, and only an occasional car whizzed by on the boulevard. Finally, there were several loud blasts, close together.

"I heard shots fired," Dellacona said later. Mattana had taken five shots in the body and one in the head, fired from a 9-mm pistol.

"Afterwards, Ventimiglia came back to the car where Russo was and they laughed and joked about it," Dellacona recalled.

Ventimiglia took pride in his having had the balls to pump the bullets into Mattana, and he later bragged about it to girlfriend Annamarie Pugliese. "There were others," he told her. "But I was the only one with enough guts to shoot him."

By this time it was the early hours of April 28, 1976.

Vicki Ardito's scheme had been carried out and her lover was dead, lying in the mud at Howard Beach, with only the seagulls to mourn him. He was murdered not for money, but because he had dared to reject Vicki Ardito.

14

The next morning, Vicki Ardito was a wreck. Mattana, she knew by now, had to be dead. She had pulled off her plan after all.

If only Ben had listened to her, none of this would have happened. But now he was out of her life forever. She felt relief—she could get on with her life without feeling like a discarded rag doll. She knew she would miss Ben—but not the Ben he had been lately. She could have helped him with his life and his career. Maybe they could even have had kids. She could have helped him become what he wanted to be. But he wouldn't bend to her wishes, and so he had paid the ultimate price. There would be time to mourn Mattana, the Ben she loved so much, but now was not that time. There were far more pressing matters to deal with.

She took a deep breath, collected her thoughts, and called a friend who was a policeman. He in turn alerted authorities.

As Vicki awaited the arrival of the police, she went over her story again and again. What she would tell them could contain only minor variations of what had really happened at Mattana's Lloyd Harbor home the night before, but they were critical variations. Which would make her a victim, not a suspect. The key differences were that she, too, had been kidnapped. And that she had never seen the culprits before.

When the police arrived, she had her story down pat. Four thugs, she told police, had burst into the house the night before. At gunpoint, they held Mattana and demanded the keys to his shop in Lynbrook. They smashed him across the face with a gun, and he began bleeding.

Mattana had the combination to the safe, but insisted and finally convinced the robbers that he didn't have the keys to the shop, that they were in the hands of his manager. Vicki said that two of the men then forced her to accompany them to the manager's house in Uniondale to get the keys, while Mattana was held in the house by the others.

After getting the keys, they drove to the motorcycle shop and cleaned out the safe. Then they returned to Mattana's house, Vicki said. They dumped her there but took Mattana with them; and they warned Vicki to stay put and stay quiet. They threatened her and told her not to call the police if she ever wanted to see Mattana again.

After several hours, Vicki said, since Mattana did not return, she called police despite the threats she'd received. The police dutifully took it all down.

The trickle of cops turned into a torrent of detectives who arrived at the scene as the morning wore on. They searched the house and surroundings. Outside, they found bloodstains in the driveway. And one detective, Albert Iannuzzi, found something else. Something Vicki had forgotten, something she should have known could spell disaster.

Iannuzzi poked around in the master bedroom not really knowing what he was looking for, but with an experienced detective's eye he slowly surveyed everything in the room. He opened up the closet and saw a plastic shopping bag on the shelf. There appeared to be nothing unusual about it until he saw a piece of paper through the plastic. It read: "Important . . . Big Plan . . . Kidnapping Wednesday A.M."

It seems almost inconceivable that Vicki could have left behind such a damning piece of evidence. Iannuzzi showed the paper to other detectives at the scene, the first hints that Vicki's story about the abduction might not be true.

Vicki was confronted with the evidence right away. The tale that she told about that piece of paper was far from convincing.

"She denied immediately that the note had anything to do with Mattana," Iannuzzi later said. "She said the note referred to a plan to kidnap her husband's girlfriend, who had been made pregnant by her husband."

Incredulous, the police asked Vicki to go on. She explained that she had been separated from Gerald Ardito, and that they were not having an easy divorce. They were fighting over money, and trying to get as much dirt on one another as they could. He had even hired a private detective, a woman. And he had an affair with her, and made her pregnant. Yet he was suing Vicki for divorce on grounds of adultery.

"But Vicki told me she had an idea of how she could counter her husband's suit," said Iannuzzi. "She told me if she got the girl kidnapped and got her to talk to Gerald Ardito on the phone, she'd get him to admit that it was his baby. Then Vicki would have him where she wanted him."

The detectives looked at one another. Even if everything Vicki had told them were true, which was hard to believe, what kind of woman did they have on their hands, one who would plan to kidnap someone to get leverage in a divorce?

The murder of Ben Mattana was only hours old, and already a thickening cloud of suspicion began to descend on Vicki Ardito.

15

As the days wore on, apprehension about Mattana's fate increased. There was no sign or word of him, nor any word from the kidnappers about a ransom. Meanwhile, at least some of Vicki's story was being corroborated by the police. The safe at Mattana's motorcycle shop was left wide open, the cash gone, and the floor was littered with papers from it. Among those papers was a New York State registration card for Vicki's Kawasaki motorcycle with some numbers written on it. The numbers were the combination to the safe.

The media was quick to get on the case. Reporters raced to the house, all the radio stations carried the story, and television crews were set up on the lawn of Mattana's home. The evening news featured Vicki on camera, making a plea to the kidnappers.

The story was a natural. There was sex—a woman with four children living with a handsome motorcycle jock ten years younger than herself. There was money—her estranged husband was a millionaire who lived in fashionable Old Westbury. And, of course, suspense—Who had committed the robbery and kidnapping? Why? And what would be the fate of Ben Mattana? It was the kind of ongoing story, with plenty of spice, that sells newspapers and rivets viewers to their TV screens.

Indeed, before the entire story unfolded, it would become the crime story of the decade on Long Island— "The Motorcycle Mama Murder Case." It had legs not only because of all the sexy ingredients, but also because the entire drama would take almost a decade to play out. And no Hollywood screenwriter would have dared give it the bizarre turns it took in reality.

Investigators continued their preliminary probe, and the more they learned the more concerned they were about Ben Mattana. One fact did not seem to click: If he had been kidnapped, who would be in a position to pay a ransom for him? His family had little money; Vicki was broke.

The only person in the whole puzzle with serious money was Gerald Ardito. But he was going through a tug-of-war divorce with Vicki over money. He'd be more likely to wish Mattana good riddance than pay any ransom for him. Could he be a suspect?

The police decided to speak to Ardito, but they were unable to locate him. His whereabouts were temporarily unknown. His whereabouts were often unknown.

With all the media attention, the Ardito children were quick to learn about what had happened to their mother and her boyfriend. They suddenly found themselves in the limelight too. They would spend years trying to escape it. It wasn't only just the unwanted attention and the whispering of schoolmates and neighbors they had to contend with, there was also the specter of physical harm. No one would be haunted by that threat more than Jed Ardito, the oldest son.

For a few days, Vicki Ardito stayed in the former chicken coop with police, staring at the telephone, waiting for a ransom call she knew would never come. And the police clocked her every move. Since the crimes committed had crossed the county lines from Nassau into Suffolk, detectives from both were involved in the case. After twenty-four hours, the requisite waiting period on alleged kidnapping cases, the FBI was brought in. In all, more than twenty investigators were on the case. And with each passing hour with no word from the kidnappers, hopes for Ben Mattana faded. And suspicions mounted that Vicki Ardito had not told them the whole story.

"I believe he was not taken for ransom," Suffolk Chief of Detectives David Buckley said. "And in view of his length of absence, foul play is a distinct possibility."

The house that Vicki had transformed into a dream home became a nightmare of a prison. Everywhere she looked there were reminders of Ben and of their happier times together; also of the last night of his life. Vicki had been living life in the fast lane for a long time and was no pussycat, but she was not a stone-cold killer either. The walls of the house began closing in, her nerves began to fray. It was beginning to sink in that the police and FBI would not just go away after a while and let things blow over.

After a few days, she could not stand being in the house any longer and moved back to Old Westbury. Her kids needed her, and she needed the security that the house could provide.

Gerald Ardito could have gloated and turned his back on his helpless, estranged wife, who had the nerve to walk out on him and embarrass him.

But now she was in a real jam and needed him. "It was a pride thing," a Long Island acquaintance recalled. "He wanted everyone to think he was a stand-up guy, who would do the right thing even though his wife had left him and disgraced him.

"It was the kind of thing mob people would do. Ardito had no connections at all with the wise guys, but he liked to let people think otherwise."

It was obvious that Vicki would also need top legal help. So Gerald looked to an old school acquaintance for suggestions. The man was James LaRossa, the New York criminal attorney Jed Ardito would turn to in his hour of desperation seventeen years later. Like mother, like son.

Vicki wasn't the only one feeling pressure. Benny Ventimiglia had to suspect that the police would eventually link him to Vicki. He had been giving Jed karate instructions and was a frequent visitor to the Old Westbury house. The police would soon learn of his criminal record and start theorizing. But he faced an even more immediate threat. There was a drug dealer on his case, and owing money to drug dealers can be fatal.

Maybe Ventimiglia was high on coke when he spoke to his dealer. Maybe he thought he could threaten him to get him off his back. Maybe he just couldn't resist the temptation to brag that he was capable of murder. But his response to the dealer indicated how much of a loose cannon he really was, and how hard it was for him to keep his mouth shut.

"Then he tells me," the dealer testified, quoting Ventimiglia, " 'I just wasted a guy myself and dumped the body in Howard Beach.' Then he wanted me to fake an alibi for him that he was in Philadephia the night of the murder, that he was there a couple of days."

Ventimiglia worried more about the drug debt than keeping a low profile with the police. He had turned over his share of the $1,500 in the safe to the dealer, to buy a little time. But he still owed more.

Instead of laying low, Ventimiglia and Russo began hounding Vicki for the $10,000 they were owed for the murder. She stalled them, saying she would pay off as soon as Mattana's house was sold. Dellacona, on the other hand, wouldn't dare go near Vicki or the other two men.

Vicki had taken Dellacona into her confidence early in her planning to kill Mattana—when she still entertained such plans as driving Mattana off a cliff, or doing him in with an overdose of cocaine. Dellacona wanted no part of it. When it became clear she would need accomplices to do the dirty deed, and that a contract hit would be safer for her, she asked Dellacona for suggestions. Dellacona had a heroin habit, and had committed burglaries and thefts to support that habit. So he suggested using a drug addict. "I want people who have done this before," she told him.

But finding experienced pros proved a lot more difficult than it seemed. And when Vicki settled on Ventimiglia, twenty, and Russo, only a kid of sixteen, she had to know the risk of getting caught was high. More than anything else, it was the thoughtless use of the telephone that did in Vicki and her novice killers.

As a matter of routine, investigators checked out telephone calls made from Mattana's house and Vicki's Old Westbury home the day of the kidnapping and robbery.

They were especially interested in calls from the Mattana home on the evening of April 27. There were several placed to numbers that had never been called from the Mattana home before and that were placed during the time of the kidnapping.

"The telephone records gave us the direction," said Gerald Sullivan, chief of the district attorney's major offenses bureau in Suffolk County.

One phone call took them directly to the home of Ventimiglia himself. The calls also led police to the home of two of Ventimiglia's girlfriends, including Ivy Furness, 20, of Oceanside, Long Island.

Suffolk Detective George Latchford spoke to Furness, who eventually confirmed to police that Vicki Ardito knew Ventimiglia and Russo. She had seen them together.

The scent began to grow stronger. At first, the other girl Ventimiglia called that evening, Annamarie Pugliese, would say little, but Latchford knew she was aware of much more than she let on and he kept on going back to her.

"I was afraid," she later said, explaining her reluctance to tell the police everything she knew.

But eventually she confirmed getting a phone call from Ventimiglia on the night of April 27—the only call she got that evening. And she also told Latchford that Ventimiglia had taught Vicki's son Jed karate in the Ardito home in Old Westbury. Eventually she would have even more to say.

Tracing other calls netted the police more confirming evidence. They checked calls made from Vicki's Old Westbury address the day of the kidnapping. Several were made to a Brooklyn pizzeria owned by the father of Mario Russo, who worked there as a counterman. The police now had plenty of circumstantial evidence, but they lacked the most important evidence of all—Ben Mattana's body.

16

Spring had always been an especially rejuvenating time for Vicki Ardito. The warmer days and extra hours of daylight meant more time for racing her various vehicles—from her trophy-winning Corvette to dune buggies to her motorcycle. The season also signaled the start of open house at the Arditos. Her racing friends would come over, hang out, putter with their engines, and generally drive Vicki's neighbors crazy.

The kids were invited to bring home their school friends, and there would be frequent parties and barbecues at which her friends would mix with those of her kids. They were not that far apart in age.

But Vicki Ardito would never know a carefree spring again. In early May 1976, she returned to live in the home of Gerald Ardito under a cloud that would only darken.

What would that confrontation have been like? Vicki standing before him, her eyes glazed, her appearance beginning to show the strain she was under. Whatever problems they had before, everything paled now. She looked at him and awaited a question that never came. Yes, she thought, that would be just like the sonofabitch to act unshockable so he'd have a chance to show his macho. Finally, she asks the question for him.

"Well, aren't you going to ask me if I had something to do with this?"

"It doesn't matter," he says. "It's all over. He's gone, screw him, whether or not you had anything to do with it."

"The cops are nosing around a lot."

"The cops have questioned me, too."

"What should I do?"

"Stay at home with your kids and get on with your life. We'll worry about the divorce later."

"Macho man. By the way, how's your private eye these days? Knocked up again?"

Gerald just grunts. "You've got your daughter's wedding to attend to, you know."

"Oh, my God," she suddenly recalls. "Dina's wedding is only a couple of weeks away."

"It's all okay. Everything is under control. Everything will go ahead as planned. It's going to be a wonderful wedding."

"Right. Wonderful."

For a few weeks, things did calm down a bit for Vicki, as the police continued running down their leads. It was the calm before the storm.

On May 26, the robbery-kidnapping officially became a murder case. On that date, the police discovered a badly decomposed body in a lot in Howard Beach. Sergeant Charles Perry of the 106th Precinct's anti-crime unit discovered the body lying on its side about 1 P.M. in a junk-filled, overgrown lot at 161st Avenue and 86th Street in Howard Beach. Although the body was too badly decomposed to allow for a ready identification, the police did not have to wait for the autopsy reports to confirm that it was Ben Mattana. They hadn't happened upon this body by accident. They were looking for Mattana, and they knew where to look.

How did they know the whereabouts of the body? The ultimate source could only have been the culprits themselves. Ventimiglia was that source.

About a week and a half after Mattana's disappearance, Annamarie Pugliese had overheard Ventimiglia talking to Russo. She eventually told police the gist of that conversation.

"Don't go near Howard Beach," Ventimiglia said, "because the police have found the body there." He was mistaken then, of course. The police had no idea where the body was.

It actually took the police weeks to find Mattana's corpse—using Ventimiglia's own words as a map.

For Annamarie Pugliese there was irony in the use of Howard Beach as the dumping ground for Ben Mattana. During the salad days of her relationship with Ventimiglia, they would sometimes go for walks in the area. But lately their romance had cooled, even before the kidnapping and murder.

"The relationship had become strained," she said. "He refused to marry me, and he was dating other women."

Ben Mattana had gotten himself killed for dumping the wrong woman; Benny Ventimiglia had gotten himself fingered for shooting off his mouth to a woman whom he had turned down.

"Hell hath no fury like a woman scorned," said Suffolk Police Commissioner Eugene Kelly at an evening press conference on June 1. At it, he announced the arrests of Vicki Ardito and John Dellacona. Warrants were also out for the arrests of Ventimiglia and Russo.

Suffolk Chief of Detectives David Buckley said that the investigation by Suffolk, Nassau, and New York City police, and FBI agents from the Chief's Babylon bureau, had broken the case. The indictment charged that Vicki had planned the whole episode and offered "a substantial amount of money to have Mattana kidnapped and killed."

The indictment charged Vicki and the other defendants with first-degree conspiracy, felony murder, kidnapping, and robbery related to the alleged theft of $1,500 from Mattana's safe.

A reporter later contacted Ventimiglia's sister-in-law, who said of him, "Everybody knows he's a good boy. Maybe somebody else did it and used his name."

At the bail hearing on June 3, Gerald Ardito came to Vicki's temporary rescue. On hand with him at the hearing was John Sutter, one of the best criminal defense attorneys in Suffolk.

Sutter asked that Vicki be freed on bail because she was a businesswoman and the mother of four children. Suffolk County Court Judge set the bail at $150,000. The bail was promptly posted, but Vicki had to wait a while before being temporarily freed. She had a few outstanding traffic warrants in Nassau County. Another $100 bond had to be posted in Valley Stream, in Nassau County, pending those charges. Finally, at 4:15 A.M. on June 3, she was released.

Gerald Ardito was asked to take the stand during the trial hearing. At one point, County Prosecutor David Clayton cross-examined Ardito, who was pleading for Vicki's release. But Clayton posed a potentially explosive question to him, not about Vicki's involvement with Mattana, but about his own.

"Did you ever make a phone call to Ben Mattana, threatening his life?" he was asked.

The question, of course, was totally out of order. Gerald Ardito had not been implicated in any way in the crimes committed, he was not the subject of the hearing, and he could not be asked to incriminate himself. But Clayton had tossed the hand grenade anyway, hoping that Ardito might blurt out something. Ardito simply remained silent, waiting for the inevitable objection from his attorney. It was sustained, of course.

One of the factors Ardito wanted the judge to take into account in determining bail was the impending wedding of their daughter Dina. The nuptials were set for the coming Saturday, June 4.

"You really want your wife to attend your daughter's wedding this Saturday, don't you?" asked Clayton, his voice dripping with sarcasm.

"Yes I do," Ardito replied. And she did.

17

Gerald Ardito had spared no expense, and pulled every string at his disposal, in arranging his daughter's church wedding.

Even though his daughter lived in Nassau County on Long Island, the wedding would be held in Manhattan. In the Catholic church, weddings normally take place in the parish where the bride-to-be resides. That wasn't good enough for Ardito.

He wanted his daughter wed at St. Ignatius Loyola Church, on 84th Street and Park Avenue. This jewel of a church is not like St. Patrick's Cathedral, a giant barn of a place where New York's most famous Catholics have their funerals. For weddings, elite Catholics prefer St. Ignatius. The church is run by the Jesuits and is named after the founder of the order. The Jesuits long have had a history for currying favor among the powerful, and their showcase church in the middle of the city's richest neighborhood was a magnet for them.

Now a millionaire and also a graduate of a Jesuit college, Gerald Ardito was able to arrange to hold the wedding at St. Ignatius—doubtless with the promise of a hefty donation. When it came to putting money in the right hands, Ardito was no cheapskate.

It was a beautiful June day, and at about 4:25 that afternoon—a fashionable 25 minutes late—the bride pulled up in front of the church in a white 1953 Bentley. Her father and mother were with her. And so were a clutch of bodyguards.

The bodyguards were there for good reason. Ventimiglia had been indicted for murder and was still at large. He had very good reason not to want Vicki around to testify at a trial. Furthermore, he had already demonstrated he was not reluctant to make threats. At the bail hearing the day before, a prosecutor had recounted how Ventimiglia had made a murder threat before. James Pape had been threatened when he happened upon Ventimiglia and the others in Mattana's home just before the murder. "If you tell anyone you saw us here, we will come back and blow your brains out," Ventimiglia had threatened.

Exiting the white Bentley in her exquisite white wedding gown, the pretty 18-year-old Dina Ardito had more than the usual complement of escorts. There were bridesmaids, of course, and ushers. And there were bodyguards. Two, formally dressed, as were most guests, were hired by Gerald Ardito. In addition, there were two New York City detectives present, and three from Suffolk County.

Indeed, someone had called in a death threat to the police the morning of the wedding. The intended victim: Vicki Ardito. But there were no incidents at the church as Dina Ardito wed Carmine Riccio, of Beverly Hills, California.

After the ceremony, Dina and her new husband, preceded and followed by bodyguards, got back into the Bentley for the 25-block ride down to the fashionable Plaza Hotel, where a lavish wedding reception was held as if no one had a care in the world. But seven bodyguards diligently stood watch.

The Suffolk County Courthouse and jail in Riverhead resembles a college campus. The buildings are clustered amidst acres of lawn and pine trees. Just across the highway the Peconic River runs by, a stream popular with canoeists and kayakers. The swinging Hamptons are just a few miles away.

On June 14, the sounds of chirping birds were quickly drowned out by the clatter of a helicopter circling overhead. Carefully the pilot set the chopper down on a small pad near the courthouse. As soon as it landed, police exited with a man wrapped in a white sheet, who was hustled inside.

Earlier that same day, Benny Ventimiglia stood in front of the mirror and considered very carefully what he would wear. It could be the last outfit he would wear as a free man for a very long time. He examined his face. He looked wan. The coke. His thin moustache didn't help. But did he look like a killer to a judge or jury? How much did they have on him anyway?

He chose his best black suit and a black silk shirt, open at the neck. He was dressed as if he were going to an Italian hoodlum's funeral. And he was—his own.

First, he went to his lawyer. A curious choice—Marvin Zewen, who was an assistant to John Sutter, the high-powered lawyer who represented Vicki Ardito. Investigators surmised there had to be a link. Gerald Ardito must have hired the lawyer for Ventimiglia, in return for no more death threats.

With Zewen in tow, Ventimiglia surrendered himself at the office of the Suffolk County District Attorney in Riverhead. Within hours he'd be before a judge at a bail hearing. But first, he had to be positively identified—by a man Ventimiglia had threatened to kill.

Out of a lineup, James Pape, helicoptered in for the occasion, promptly made the ID. Police were concerned enough about Pape's safety that they had flown him in and covered him with a sheet. Even though Ventimiglia was in custody and couldn't harm anybody. It was clear the police felt that Ventimiglia had some friends who might owe him favors.

Ventimiglia faced the judge stonily at the bail hearing as the prosecutor, David W. Clayton, argued against bail.

"Despite his young age," he said, pointing to the 20-year-old Ventimiglia, "he has a robbery conviction in Queens for which he has been paroled . . . and [he has] been a fugitive from justice for two weeks. We would oppose the setting of any bail on him."

Zewen did not even ask that any bail be set. He did say, however, that his client had matchbooks to confirm he had been in California at the time. No bail was allowed, and Benny Ventimiglia was led to jail.

But just two weeks later, Benny would get another chance to get free on bail. And this time he wouldn't be represented by Sutter's number two, Marvin Zewen, but by Sutter himself. This time, over the objections of prosecutor Clayton, bail was set at $100,000. The bail money would be forthcoming—doubtless from Gerald Ardito.

At the bail hearing, a tentative date of September 9 was set for the trial of Ventimiglia, Vicki Ardito, and John Dellacona. The fourth suspect, Mark Russo, was still at large. All out on bail—$150,000 for Vicki, $100,000 for Ventimiglia, and $20,000 for Dellacona—the trio had a long summer to get their cases ready. And then some.

For the accused, the case was hardly hopeless. Over the next few months, their defense attorneys would see that the case against them rested largely on circumstantial evidence. There were no direct witnesses, there was no murder weapon. There was one thing that bothered them a lot, however, and that was the statements which Benny Ventimiglia had given to Detective Lieutenant Walter Cunningham and FBI Special Agent Walter Distler. They had grilled him for six hours on May 12. Although Benny didn't know it, his statements had been tape-recorded. The taping device was hidden inside a phone. What he'd said to them was damaging to his defense, but there was a legal question about whether those statements could be introduced into evidence, because Benny didn't know about the bug.

September 9 came and went without a trial. There was one delay after another, and ultimately the trial would not start until February 1977. But first there would be an evidentiary hearing concerning the admissibility of Benny's taped statements; that hearing began in late October 1976. By then, Ventimiglia had his own exclusive team of expensive attorneys, Thomas Hession and Ronald Bekoff. They argued that since Benny had not been advised of his rights, the taped statements should not be admissible. The judge ruled in Ventimiglia's favor.

While attorneys for the defense could take heart in having succeeded in barring Ventimiglia's statements from the trial, they soon had reason to fear the worst.

Prosecutors had been trying for months to get John Dellacona to turn. He said he had had nothing to do with the murder. Prosecutors said they would be willing to get him a separate trial if he would testify against the others.

Dellacona was a drug addict who had committed robberies to support his habit, but he insisted he wasn't a killer and would be damned if he'd share the rap with the real killers. If Dellacona consented to the deal and agreed to testify, the case for the defense would be bleak indeed.

Pretty Marie Daniele was 24 when Jed Ardito strangled her to death in a Manhattan hotel room.
(*New York Post*)

Frances (Vicki) Ardito, the mother who had her lover kidnapped and killed. (*New York Post*/Vic DeLucia)

Gerald (Jed) Ardito, the son who choked his lover to death. (*New York Post*/Charles Wenzelberg)

Sebastian (Benny) Ventimiglia killed Vicki's lover Ben Mattana, Jr. and taught her son Jed karate. (*New York Post*)

Vicki Ardito was all smiles at her trial for the murder of Ben Mattana, Jr. in 1977. (Bob Luckey/*Newsday*)

Vicki's long fight to stay out of prison finally ended in 1984; she died three years later.
(*New York Post*/Vic DeLucia)

The Grand Hyatt and the Sun Garden Restaurant (above street level), where Jed and Marie often met for lunch and had their final, fatal encounter on April 28, 1993. (Author's Collection)

Room 3431 at the Grand Hyatt, where Jed choked Marie to death. (Author's Collection)

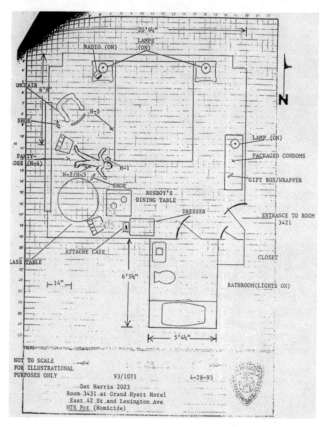

Illustration of crime scene.
(Author's Collection)

Jed Ardito is escorted from the Midtown South Precinct in
Manhattan after being charged with the death of
Marie Daniele. (John Paraskevas/*Newsday*)

Courtroom artist's sketch of Jed Ardito at his sentencing
on December 12, 1994. Judge Franklin Gould sentenced
Ardito to 8 1/3 to 25 years and recommended no parole.
(Author's Collection)

Angie and Ralph Daniele, the parents of the victim, at Ardito's sentencing. (*New York Post*/Don Halasy)

The front page of the *New York Post* of November 17, 1994, the day after Ardito was found guilty of manslaughter but not murder. (Author's Collection)

Jackie O and RFK: Author's startling claim
Pages 4, 5 & 29

NEW YORK POST
LATE CITY FINAL

FUROR OVER ROUGH SEX VERDICT

Millionaire beats murder charge

Full story: Page 3

Post Interactive: TV and your PC

18

In February 1977, at the Suffolk County Courthouse in Riverhead, the trial of Vicki Ardito, Benny Ventimiglia, and Mario Russo finally got underway. Russo had remained a fugitive until December 1, 1976, when he surrendered to the Nassau County police.

But conspicuously absent from the row of defendants was John Dellacona. Prosecutors had indeed succeeded in turning him; he would testify against the others. He would be tried later, to reduced charges, in return for his testimony. He was also allowed to remain out on bail, and had been furnished with a new identity. The former heroin addict had also been enrolled in a drug treatment program and was now on methadone.

Defense attorneys did what they could to discredit Dellacona's testimony, and they made it clear to the jury that Dellacona had made a deal with the District Attorney to save his own skin. They also pointed out that Dellacona's statements would have to be corroborated. Nonetheless, his four-day testimony was crushing to the defense. After all, he'd been there—he could identify all the players, and he had seen everything but the actual shooting. He did, however, hear the shots fired, and had also seen the two men escort the victim into the marshes and return without him.

The motive for the crime, prosecutors said, was revenge. Vicki had Mattana killed simply because he wanted to end their relationship, a relationship which had been one-sided from the beginning. Mattana was no saint, but he was open and honest with her and was, prosecutors alleged, a victim of his own kindness. They claimed that Vicki had instigated their relationship. She had bought a motorcycle for her husband in 1972 from Mattana at his Lynbrook Harley-Davidson dealership. At the time, Mattana was separated from his wife. It was at Vicki's urging that the pair started seeing one another, and in late 1974 Vicki separated from her husband and moved into Mattana's house.

Yes, Mattana was a man who liked to party and used drugs like cocaine. And, yes, he loved his freedom, which included freedom to see other women. But he was upfront with Vicki about how he felt. Several times during the months they lived together he even moved out of his own house, insisting that their affair was over. But he was not abusive to her, the attorneys said.

Mattana's brother Ronald took the stand to testify that Ben had not treated Vicki cruelly at all. "He felt it was kind of his fault she had fallen in love with him . . . he drew her away from her family. She could stay there under his terms. He could do whatever he wanted to do."

Sitting there in the Riverhead courtroom, listening to the testimony of prosecution witnesses, Vicki started to become visibly disturbed. A lifelong lover of speed and freedom, there was nowhere for her to escape, nowhere she could go. Her entire world was closing in on her fast and would inevitably lead to a prison cell.

The prosecution would take seven weeks to present its

case, calling 52 witnesses. Each day the noose grew tighter around the necks of Vicki and her accomplices.

Ventimiglia's case collapsed when Annamarie Pugliese, his former girlfriend, took the stand. She testified about getting a phone call from Ventimiglia while the crime was being committed. She testified that he asked her to lie for him, to say he had gone to Philadelphia. She further said that he confessed "that he had been the triggerman," and that "he was the only one with enough guts to shoot him [Mattana]."

Ventimiglia and Russo were doomed. But Vicki's role in Mattana's kidnapping and murder still had to be corroborated. There was only one witness who could do just that.

James Pape, Mattana's neighbor, took the stand and described how he had been threatened the night of the kidnapping. Then he blew Vicki's last alibi to pieces.

During the fatal evening of April 27, when Vicki and Mattana were at a friend's house watching the wrestling matches, Vicki called the Mattana house several times. Telephone records showed that the calls had been placed to the Mattana home. Vicki said that she was calling Pape, whom she asked to come over to the house to feed the dog. But Pape testified he was not in the house at that time and never spoke to Vicki on the phone. It was the last straw for Vicki.

In his summation, Chief Prosecutor Gerald Sullivan waved Ben Mattana's bloody shirt in front of the jury. "Corroboration," he said, "is what this represents. Dellacona said he had heard five or six shots while he was waiting for Ventimiglia and Mario Russo in Howard Beach. The shirt has four or five holes in it; another bullet was fired into Mattana's head."

The gesture was dramatic, and effective. But Vicki Ardito was not in the courtroom to see it. In the closing days of the trial, she seemed disoriented. Her normally well-groomed appearance had given way to a lean and haggard look. She complained of not sleeping, and her eyes were like saucers. She hardly looked the part of a "Motorcycle Mama" who was making it with younger men.

Finally, her behavior became so erratic she couldn't make it to the courtroom at all, and was confined to Mount Sinai Hospital in Manhattan. Her lawyer said she was "emotionally drained and unable to continue."

A doctor who examined her reported she had something wrong with her intestines, and was suffering from extreme emotional anxiety. Her sudden illness, in the closing days of the trial, was deemed very suspicious.

Judge Thomas M. Stark wouldn't buy it. After a few days' delay, he insisted Vicki be brought into court. Her outfit was a far cry from the tight pants and halter tops she used to wear. She was a mess—ashen faced, with no makeup at all. Her gray hair stood out wildly. She was wearing pajamas, slippers, and a fur coat.

Stark still was unconvinced. He canceled her bail and sentenced her to the Central Suffolk Hospital in Riverhead for a physical examination. "This lady is faking!" he fumed.

But three days later, Vicki appeared in court looking even worse. She wore the same outfit. But she was visibly weaker. Her lawyers had to help her to her chair, and then she slumped over on the table. She paid no attention to the proceedings and appeared lost in a faraway world.

Presenting testimony from psychiatrists who said that she was suffering from mental illness, Vicki's lawyers asked that she be committed for long-term psychiatric care. Judge Stark ordered her sent to the Mid-Hudson

Psychiatric Center, near Poughkeepsie, New York, for a period not to exceed one year. Vicki's case was declared a mistrial, and all testimony in the case against her was stricken from the record.

Benny Ventimiglia went out with a flourish. The jury found him guilty of kidnapping and murder, and he was sentenced to 25 years to life. Mario Russo was also found guilty and sentenced to 20 years to life. He had provided the gun for the shooting, but didn't pull the trigger.

At the sentencing April 19, prosecutor Gerald Sullivan got in his final jabs at Ventimiglia.

"This defendant has no right to ask for more mercy than he granted Mattana. Mattana begged for his life and this man laughed and shot him. He has no remorse . . . he has no perception of the value of human life. . . . He is a menace to the community."

Judge Thomas M. Stark added his comments from the bench. He said that Ventimiglia had been given a break when he was allowed to plead guilty to single counts of robbery and grand larceny, when he had been indicted in Brooklyn and Queens on 14 armed-robbery holdups. "You were on probation less than a year when you committed this crime," Stark snarled. "You were the director of this, you yourself put bullets into Ben Mattana and then bragged about it."

Ventimiglia appeared unmoved. The courthouse that day was crowded with friends of the late Ben Mattana, who had come to show their support for his family and contempt for his killer. As Ventimiglia was being led in cuffs out of the courtroom, they cheered. Seizing the moment, Ventimiglia smiled, and raised his cuffed, clasped hands in the air—as if in triumph. The cheers quickly changed to taunts and insults.

Ventimiglia was to have a busy day before settling

down to begin his sentence. First, there was an appearance to be made in Southampton Town Court, where he pleaded guilty to smuggling marijuana into jail while he was on trial.

Then he was whisked off to another court in Queens, where he faced other criminal charges. Sebastian (Benny) Ventimiglia, Long Island's one-man crime wave, was 21 years old.

His conviction was appealed, and on a point of law Sebastian (Benny) Ventimiglia would achieve lasting fame in the court system of New York. He has a legal proceeding named after him: The Ventimiglia Hearing.

In his appeal, the defense charged that testimony was admitted into the trial which should not have been. The testimony consisted of statements made by Ventimiglia about where they stashed the body. "Where we put people and they haven't found them for weeks and months."

The defense charged such a statement was inadmissible, since it implies admission of prior murders, murders that have nothing to do with this case.

But the state's highest court, the Court of Appeals, ruled that the statements were indeed admissible, "since their probative value as to premeditation of murder and as to plan of conspiracy, outweighed prejudice resulting from implicit admission that the defendants' committed prior murders. . . ."

The decision was historic, and to this day all similar hearings are known as Ventimiglia hearings. At them, judges decide whether evidence can be allowed if it implies another, previous bad act by the defendant. It's often a tough decision, and the ruling can determine the outcome of a case.

It would be at a Ventimiglia hearing, many years later, that Jed Ardito would sweat out such a decision—at a hearing named after the man who had taught him karate, and carried out his mother's murder scheme.

John Dellacona was rewarded handsomely by the arbiters of justice for testifying against his three co-conspirators. In January 1978, a quiet trial was held before a judge, not a jury. Dellacona's attorney, Harvey Aronoff, claimed that his client had been been forced to participate in the slaying. "A defense of duress was asserted," said Aronoff. Judge Lawrence J. Bracken agreed. John Dellacona was acquitted on all counts.

Vicki stayed at the Mid-Hudson Psychiatric Center for a year before another hearing was held, in May 1978, to determine if she was then able to stand trial. The hearing was held before the same Justice Thomas M. Stark, who had presided over the murder case.

The hearing took four days, during which five psychiatrists testified that Vicki was suffering from mental disease, although opinions differed as to which one.

Prosecutor Gerald Sullivan was not buying any of it. He questioned the experts at length about hospital reports that Ardito regularly ordered food from outside the hospital and sponsored pizza parties for other patients on her ward. Sullivan put another psychiatrist and a clinical psychologist on the stand. They both testified that Vicki was malingering and was fit to stand trial for murder.

Throughout the entire hearing, Vicki remained slumped over a table, seemingly oblivious to all going on around her. Judge Stark finally ruled in favor of the five psychiatrists and ordered Vicki sent back to Mid-Hudson for another year. Among the disorders Vicki was said to be suffering from were agitated depression, hysterical neurosis, manic depression, and schizophrenia. She would spend the next several years in psychiatric hospitals.

19

If Vicki Ardito was feigning mental illness, it was an Oscar-winning performance. For years, she was able to convince teams of psychiatrists that she was emotionally unable to defend herself in court.

Of course her chief prosecutor, Gerald Sullivan, and her trial judge, Thomas Stark, never believed it for a minute. But this was the late seventies, the high-water mark of psychiatrists' clout in the criminal justice system. They were the social science geniuses of the moment, and their explanations and rationalizations of why good people did bad things carried a lot of weight with juries and liberal judges. Terrible acts committed by normally sane and sober people were aberrational, they maintained, and could somehow be explained or excused. Something must have snapped. The individual was not really responsible for the crime; her husband, or mother, or father, or environment, or even the consumption of a Twinkie, could be the cause. Blame was placed everywhere but on the culprit, and victims were forgotten.

If you had any kind of talent at all, your crime—even murder—could simply be pardoned. In 1981 Norman Mailer went on a crusade to free a killer named Jack Abbott. Writers do this periodically—take up the cudgels for the "wrongfully convicted;" it enhances their reputations.

There was no doubt Abbott was a killer—he had killed an inmate in prison. But he could string sentences together and had written powerful letters to Mailer. Mailer, who himself had once jabbed one of his ex-wives with a small knife, crusaded to get him paroled. He has had blood on his hands ever since.

Thanks at least in part to the author, Abbott was set free. Abbott became the darling of the liberal literary set, more impressed with his powers of description than destruction. Yet he had clearly telegraphed what his next move would be, in his grisly book titled *In the Belly of the Beast*, in which he describes the "gentleness of the feeling at the center of a coarse act of murder." Abbott was not long out of prison before he relieved that sick feeling. He stabbed to death a young immigrant waiter outside a food shop on Second Avenue. His literary talents notwithstanding, Abbott was returned to jail.

Mailer was apologetic. "My culpability was assuming I was the one who was in danger. And I wasn't. The one who was in danger was the first stranger who cut across his bow in the wrong way. It's a sad, sad, sad, sour story."

But it was a liberal era, and establishment norms about crime and punishment and accountability were being attacked. The psychiatrists had an explanation for almost everything, and the courts listened. And money could buy a roomful of experts—who would happily dance to the tune of the purchaser. They were like Vicki's chimpanzees, performing for bananas.

It was Vicki's hope that eventually she would walk out of a mental institution—not to stand trial, but as a free woman. All she had to do was convince the psychiatrists that she had been insane, by their own definition, when she had Mattana killed. And that since then, she had been cured.

She could have taken her cue from Jack Nicholson, the celluloid hero of the day, who in 1976 won an Oscar for his role in *One Flew Over the Cuckoo's Nest*. The movie caught the spirit of the time and was a smash at the box office. It won five major academy awards—Best Picture, Best Director, Best Screenplay, Best Actress, and Best Actor. No motion picture in more than forty years had won as many major awards. It brilliantly conveyed a message that people wanted to believe. That likable, talented people should not have to be held fully accountable for their mistakes, that they should be forgiven, not incarcerated. Society was at fault; not the wrongdoer.

Nicholson, in his best performance ever, played the part of a character with the preposterous name of Randle P. McMurphy, a lovable scoundrel whose naughty behavior has landed him in prison. Never mind what he did to get there. The film doesn't concern itself with that. But McMurphy balks at the idea of going to a prison work farm, and feigns madness. He opts for the nuthouse over the workhouse. Poor choice. For the mental ward to which he is assigned to is run by the wicked Nurse Ratched (played by Louise Fletcher). A mean, self-righteous bitch, she is more than a match for McMurphy. But McMurphy is a charmer, and manipulates the loony inmates, disrupting the rigid order Nurse Ratched has imposed. Her orchestrated herd soon becomes unmanageable. The audience roots against her and for the impish McMurphy and the wardful of pathetic madmen.

There is a marvelous, hilarious scene where McMurphy springs the inmates and somehow gets them on a fishing boat to catch salmon. Improbably, they return to the dock with their arms full of fish. Even more improbably,

McMurphy, like a good boy scout leader, returns them all, and himself, to the mental ward.

But Nurse Ratched is still very much in charge, and McMurphy cannot control his frustration with her any longer. He physically attacks her, to the delight of the audience. But when he is finally restrained, the fiendish Nurse Ratched seizes her opportunity to have his brain sliced up. She convinces doctors to perform a lobotomy on McMurphy (a barbaric surgical procedure abandoned long before the film was made). The operation renders McMurphy an imbecile.

It remains for the Indian giant, Chief Bromden, to perform the coup de grâce on McMurphy. He liberates McMurphy from his blissful ignorance by smothering him to death with a pillow. The chief then goes over the wall—he is the one who flies over the cuckoo's nest. And that would be Vicki Ardito's goal.

Vicki spent six long years in psychiatric hospitals. If it was true that she occasionally threw pizza parties for her fellow patients, maybe she was like McMurphy taking the inmates on a fishing trip.

But this was no movie with a fantasy ending. There may have been some light moments, but no mental hospital is a holiday camp. If Vicki wasn't really off her rocker when she was first committed to a prison hospital, her mental health certainly wasn't improved by what she encountered once she arrived.

Yet in her time in prison hospitals, there was a sea change in the way courts treated emotionally disturbed defendants. The change came about because of the attempted assassination of Ronald Reagan by John Hinckley in 1982.

Hinckley tried to kill Reagan because he was obsessed with actress Jodie Foster and wanted to impress her.

Surely, his lawyers said, he was mentally incompetent when he went on his shooting spree, and was unfit to stand trial. His fate could have been a few years of therapy in a mental hospital and then, once the psychiatrists pronounced him cured, freedom to to walk the streets again.

But Hinckley had shot the president, a conservative one at that. And he'd also shot Reagan's press secretary, James Brady, causing him permanent brain damage. There was no way the courts would be allowed to assign Hinckley to a short-term hospital stay. The influence of psychiatrists in the courtroom was diminished with the rap of a judge's gavel. Hinckley was found insane, but there was no possibility he would be set free for many, many years, if ever.

"Within three years of the Hinckley verdict," observed Lincoln Caplan in *New York* magazine, "the federal government and 34 states had changed their laws—mainly to shift the burden of proof to defendants but mainly to make it easier to keep not-guilty-by-reason-of-insanity defendants in custody."

But for a few years, at least, Vicki could cling to the hope of eventual freedom. And that hope sustained her.

Her first mental home was the high-security Mid-Hudson Psychiatric Center, in New Hampton, New York, near Poughkeepsie. After a stint at Mid-Hudson, and after having been periodically judged mentally unfit to stand trial, Vicki got a big break. She was transferred to South Beach Psychiatric Center, on Staten Island, smack in the middle of New York City.

Ordinarily, Vicki would have been sent to one of the state psychiatric centers on Long Island. The aptly named South Beach facility was a resort in comparison. The transfer was so unusual that Suffolk Assistant District Attorney Michael Ahearn later testified that the only explanation could be political pressure. Some officials suspected the hand of her ex-husband, Gerald, who was said to be a big contributor to Mario Cuomo's political war chest. Her assignment certainly was atypical.

At South Beach, Vicki was only one of about 20 criminal patients, out of a population of about 310. She was the only one from Long Island. The hospital was more like a campus than a prison, and patients could freely roam the grounds, to walk, to take in some fresh air, to gaze at the tall buildings of Manhattan just across the river. After all, most of the patients were not criminals.

Though there was a chain-link fence around the hospital, topped with barbed wire, the gate to the hospital was of the railroad-crossing type, and manned by a single guard. The facility was hardly escape-proof.

But Vicki made no attempt to flee in the 3½ years she was at South Beach. She had little reason to. For one thing, she was actually allowed to go home on occasion, totally unsupervised. Between November 1981 and September 1982, she was routinely granted 40-hour passes, enabling her to visit her family, then living in Huntington, Long Island. She was often able to string together several 40-hour passes, which allowed her to take long weekends home.

That a woman who had been charged with masterminding her lover's kidnapping and murder would be allowed such freedom didn't seem to bother administrators at the hospital.

Of course, every time Vicki left that thinly guarded gate at South Beach, she knew she had to return. But as she rode the Staten Island ferry towards Manhattan on her passes, filling her lungs with the salt-tinged air of New York Harbor and watching the seagulls skim over the ferry's wake, she was sustained by hope. The possibility began to look better and better that one day she would never have to take a ferry ride back to South Beach.

There was a chance that her status could be changed to that of a civil patient. It would have been the first step in getting the murder charges against her dismissed, and paving the way for her unconditional release.

The proposal to change Vicki's status finally worked its way through the courts. But this was the post-Hinckley era. On June 1, 1983, Vicki's hopes for freedom were dashed when State Supreme Court Justice Richard Goldberg ruled on her application. "The conclusion in inescapable," Goldberg ruled. "Mrs. Ardito is feigning illness to avoid going to trial. This court concludes that the defendant is presently capable of understanding the nature of of the charges against her . . . and is competent to stand trial." Civil status was out of the question. The sea change in the courts had carried Vicki closer to the jailhouse steps.

The very next day, in Riverhead, State Supreme Court Justice Thomas Stark was quick to act. He had accused Vicki six years earlier of faking her mental illness, and now he had the ruling he needed to put her back on trial. He immediately signed a warrant for her arrest on the murder and kidnapping charges. Whatever dream Vicki had of walking out of South Beach a free woman vanished like a rock dropped into the river nearby.

On the following Saturday evening, Vicki had two visitors, her daughter Dina and her sister, Rosemary Rena, of Huntington, Long Island.

Four days after the judge ruled her fit to be be tried, a Sunday, Vicki went out for a stroll. She had one-hour grounds privileges, which permitted her to go about unescorted. She had a lot on her mind. She had read a copy of a Staten Island newspaper, which reported that her application for civil status had been turned down. It also reported that Judge Stark had issued a warrant for her arrest. The dreaded trial, and real prison, awaited her.

The crime was already seven years behind her, but wouldn't go away. Vicki knew what lay ahead—she'd sat through many weeks of her own trial before—and couldn't face it. She told several patients on Saturday and Sunday that "she wasn't going to return to Suffolk County or Central Islip State Hospital." Those who knew her realized that she always meant what she said, however strange it may have sounded. She said she would race cars, she said she would raise chimps, she said she would kill her lover. And she was a woman of her word.

About 8 P.M. that June evening she went for a walk on the grounds, and just kept right on going. Vicki Ardito flew out of the cuckoo's nest.

20

Hospital officials were red-faced about Vicki's having flown the coop; Suffolk authorities were furious.

Judge Stark, who had never really believed Vicki was mentally ill, said that he would order an immediate competency hearing once she was found. It was a moot point. As Assistant District Attorney Michael Ahearn pointed out, there was no doubt now she was sane enough to stand trial.

"The fact that she could read and understand the legal implications of the article should have a bearing on her competency to stand trial," Ahearn stated. "That's a piece of evidence that should be brought before the court."

If officials sounded confident about her being found soon, they had good reason. Suffolk and New York City police were already combing Staten Island, after receiving several anonymous tips "from people who said they knew where she was." But their confidence was misplaced. Those tips turned up nothing. For someone who had been incarcerated for over six years because of mental problems, Vicki still had enough cunning—and help—to give authorities the slip.

Some feared the worst, that she might have taken her

own life. Just before she vanished, her therapist at South Beach, Leslie Verter, had even ordered hospital personnel to watch for "any change in her behavior or mental status, her emotional condition." No such changes were observed, he said, and "she was not considered a danger to herself or others. We do not consider her homicidal or suicidal," he said.

But whether or not there was any emotional change in Vicki that weekend—and of course there had to be— hospital personnel were hardly in a position to say. They had not even "watched" her carefully enough to prevent her from blithely strolling off the property.

Gerald and Dina Ardito were worried about what might have happened to Vicki. They said she should have been watched more closely for a suicide attempt, because she had been caught once before hoarding pills in an attempt to store up a lethal overdose. Ira Kleiman, a spokesman for the hospital, said he could find no record of such an attempt in the hospital records during the 3½ years Vicki had been a patient at South Beach.

"I fear for my mother's well being," Dina said. "I also fear foul play by certain interested parties. I cannot understand why the authorities did not watch my mother more closely."

Of course, those same authorities the Arditos now accused of being lax were the same ones they applauded for letting Vicki take long, unsupervised passes.

The trial quickly grew cold; Vicki had disappeared without a trace. Long Island *Newsday*, which had been covering the Ardito case closely ever since 1976, saw fit to editorialize on the Vicki's flight.

"Why was Frances Victoria Ardito, whose home was in Huntington, sent to Staten Island's South Beach Psychiatric Center in the first place? Why was she permitted to leave the hospital grounds on extended passes for almost a year in violation of departmental procedures? Why weren't the Suffolk County police of the Suffolk district attorney informed of those passes, as state law demands? And when she disappeared, why were the wrong law enforcement agencies notified?"

Like most editorials, this one, too, was ignored.

But the various authorities continued to make mistakes. Several weeks after Vicki's sudden departure, a young female therapist named Michelle Fischer quit the facility. Employees come and go all the time from hospitals, especially mental hospitals. But a little checking would have disclosed that Michelle knew Vicki. In fact, she had let the 47-year-old Vicki use her apartment.

Had the police done some homework and discovered their relationship, and then kept tabs on Michelle Fischer, she would have led them straight to Vicki. For she had left her job to go and live with her.

Instead, for the next nine months, police and FBI officials only alerted agencies around the country to keep an eye out for Vicki. She was hardly a high priority.

But they did know that Vicki's mother and aunt lived in Tampa, Florida, so that area got special attention. And that's where they finally found her, after checking telephone and bank records. Vicki was living with the former hospital worker. She had dyed her hair red, and cut it short, but that fooled no one.

At 3 P.M. on March 29, 1984, Vicki's sabbatical ended. Detectives from the Manatee County Sheriff's Office and the FBI arrested her in her apartment. To supplement the money her mother had been giving her, she had been working as a housecleaner and baby-sitter. One can only guess at the reactions of parents who hired Vicki to tend their kids, and then read in the local newspapers that their baby-sitter was a suspected killer on the lam from a mental hospital.

Vicki was finally brought back to the place she hated most on earth, Riverhead, to appear yet again before her nemesis, State Supreme Court Justice Thomas M. Stark. It had been seven years since she was dragged out of his court toward the end of her first trial, and Stark was waiting for her.

This time, she had a new lawyer, Michael Pollina, who tried to arrange a plea bargain for her. Pollina said Vicki would be willing to settle for a 15-year sentence. Because so much time had elapsed—almost eight years—since the kidnapping and murder of Ben Mattana, holding another trial would have been costly and time consuming. Witnesses had moved or died, and their recollections would naturally be hazier, if they could be forced to testify again at all. A plea bargain certainly made sense. But Judge Stark stubbornly insisted on a 17-year sentence.

No compromise could be reached, and once again Stark set a trial date for Vicki, who if found guilty could have received 25 years to life, the same sentence meted out to her co-conspirator, Benny Ventimiglia.

The date was set for October 17, 1984, in Riverhead. Vicki's attorney Pollina said that he would offer a defense of "extreme emotional disturbance." Given the new attitude of the courts to mental competency, it was hardly a strong one. However, that defense, based on psychiatric evidence, would allow a jury to assign a manslaughter conviction, instead of murder. Her sentence could have been a lot shorter than the 25-to-life term that is mandatory in New York for murder. Both sides cranked up for a lengthy trial. The date was again postponed.

Finally, on October 30, 1984, Vicki and her lawyer appeared before the determined Judge Stark and once again considered the plea option. Vicki vacillated about whether to go ahead with the trial, or accept a plea, now 18 years. Early in the day, she agreed to accept that plea, and went into Judge Stark's chambers to discuss the details with the judge and her attorney, Pollina.

As she did so, Michelle Fischer, the former therapist who had lived with Vicki, sat outside in the courtroom, hurt and fuming. Fischer didn't want Vicki to accept a plea. There was still a decent chance she'd get a lesser sentence from a jury, or even beat the case entirely—as remote a chance as that may have been.

Suddenly, Vicki changed her mind. She'd chance it— hadn't Michelle taken chances for her? Word quickly spread throughout the courthouse that she had decided to stand trial after all, and jury selection was slated to begin at about 2 P.M.

But cold reality began to set in once again. The judge and her lawyer had to remind Vicki that she could wind up with an even stiffer sentence by going to trial. And her lawyer also had to know that the "emotionally disturbed" defense was a harder card to play than it would have been years earlier.

There was another reason Vicki reconsidered the plea—her daughter Dina. Dina had been arrested for dealing cocaine, and faced a long jail sentence. Prosecutors had told Vicki that if she would accept a plea in her case, the authorities would go easy on Dina. Maybe that deal was still alive.

Once again, Vicki changed her mind, for the final time. Outside, Michelle Fischer got word of Vicki's decision and did not take it well.

Behind closed doors in the courtroom, Judge Stark instructed Vicki in the procedures necessary to entering a plea. As he did so, Fischer peeked through the crack in the doors and shouted, "Vicki, don't do it! Don't plead! They're all lying to you!"

It was all in vain. Judge Stark was furious at the intrusion and asked court officers to bar Fischer from the courtroom. But a few minutes later, when the courtroom doors were opened, Fischer tried to push her way in. "You can't stop me!" she yelled. She was promptly charged with obstructing governmental administration and disorderly conduct.

Accepting the plea meant that Vicki had to verbally confess to the crimes of which she had been accused. The string had finally run out, and justice would be served. She stood meekly before the judge, resigned but not tearful. One long ordeal was finally coming to an end.

Stark asked her for a plea.

"Guilty," she said in a soft voice.

"Tell the judge what you did," Pollina instructed her.

"I hired Benny Ventimiglia to kidnap and kill Mr. Mattana. Benjamin Mattana," she quickly corrected. It was probably the only time in her life she had referred to Mattana as "Mister," as if he were some stranger. By now, of course, he was. He had been dead for over eight years.

She pleaded guilty to all of the charges against her: intentional murder, felony murder, kidnapping, and conspiracy. Subtracting the time she had already served in mental institutions, that meant Vicki would be eligible for parole in about 11 years, at best. If granted parole—and there were no guarantees—that would mean that Vicki would have been free in the fall of 1994—just in time to attend her son Jed's murder trial.

Outside the courthouse, a reporter caught up with Michelle Fischer. The former therapist said that Vicki was getting a raw deal and had been abused as a teenager. "She has had a hell of a life," she said. It wouldn't get any better.

21

Vicki Ardito was sent to Bedford Hills Correctional Facility in Westchester, New York, to serve out a sentence she would not outlive. But she would go down fighting to the last.

She would not lack for good company. One of her fellow inmates was her daughter Dina, who despite what Vicki had believed, was convicted and given a jail sentence for dealing cocaine. The prosecutors replied that Vicki had waited too long to plead guilty.

Vicki was incensed, and vowed to fight the authorities she felt had lied to her. She would try to withdraw her guilty plea.

But her grounds would not just be that Dina got jail time, even after Vicki confessed; she had another ace up her sleeve. She charged that her husband, Gerald Ardito, actually was behind the crime.

This was the first time Gerald Ardito had been seriously implicated in the case. And the thread that tied him in with the crime was tenuous indeed.

The attorney who had negotiated the guilty plea for Vicki, Michael Pollina, had since died. Vicki charged that Pollina also represented Gerald Ardito.

According to Vicki's new lawyers, Jeffrey Burns and

Lawrence Berger, Pollina knew of evidence to support Gerald Ardito's involvement. He had interviewed Benny Ventimiglia in prison. In that interview, the lawyers charged, Ventimiglia indicated that Gerald, not his wife, gave him the money to do away with Mattana. But Pollina refused to hand over notes from that conversation to Vicki's new lawyers when they asked for them.

On the bench entertaining the plea was a familiar face to Vicki, Judge Thomas Stark. He certainly knew the case well. From the outset it had been full of surprises.

Indeed, only weeks earlier, Vicki Ardito had appeared before him yet again, this time asking for permission to get married!

While she had been in the Suffolk County Jail, Vicki had met an inmate with a 15-year record of assaults and thefts, who was a Muslim. "I love him very much," she told the judge. "I can't see how I am doing anyone any harm."

She said that she had even converted to the Islamic faith in a ceremony in the jail. The chief trial prosecutor opposed the marriage, and it never took place.

Now here was Vicki back before Stark again, only weeks later, claiming that her ex-husband, Gerald was really the one responsible for the death of Ben Mattana. Could Gerald Ardito really have been involved? Stark must have thought back to the very first time Vicki stood before him at the bail hearing. Gerald testified in her behalf, so she could attend her daughter's wedding. But during questioning, the assistant prosecutor asked Gerald what seemed like an outrageous question: Had Ardito himself threatened Ben Mattana. Gerald Ardito never answered that question of course. His lawyer's objection was quickly sustained. But what if . . .?

Indeed, there had been an incident, way back in 1975, that suggested Gerald Ardito might have threatened Mattana. And Vicki now made the most of it in making her plea. On December 19, 1975, there was a record of a confrontation between Gerald Ardito and Ben Mattana, which was reported by police in Lloyd Harbor, Long Island.

Mattana told police at the time that Gerald had threatened him with a gun in the converted chicken coop where Mattana lived. But police found no weapon, and marked down the incident as a family disturbance.

But on the witness stand, Vicki now claimed that there had been "a shootout." (Outside the courtroom, Vicki's lawyers elaborated to a reporter that Gerald Ardito had gone into Mattana's home with a pistol in his hand, that Mattana grabbed a gun of his own, and that there was an exchange of gunfire, but no one was injured. Gerald Ardito had then fled, they said.)

Vicki testified that because of the shootout she then hid Mattana's gun, leaving him unarmed when the masked men came and kidnapped him four months later.

"I am not guilty . . . Gerald Ardito . . . was the moving force and mastermind behind the crimes for which I am currently charged," Vicki said in her six-page affidavit seeking a new trial. She said that she learned that Benny Ventimiglia was "bought and paid for" by her ex-husband only after her lawyer told her that Ventimiglia said so.

Stark promised to give the matter some thought. "I believe such issues are raised that the defendant should have an opportunity to present evidence in support of her claim." Stark set a hearing date a few weeks hence.

But what evidence could be presented?

But, temporarily at least, the case was still alive. There was still a chance Vicki would be able to get out of prison. Like all new inmates, she had to cling to that thread of hope, as slender as it was, or sink into despair.

Although she had received a lot of press attention,

Vicki was not the best-known inmate at Bedford Hills. Also serving time there when she arrived was Jean Harris, the former headmistress who had been convicted of killing Dr. Herman Tarnower, a cardiologist and internist, and the author of the bestselling book, *The Complete Scarsdale Medical Diet*. Vicki Ardito and Jean Harris had come from totally different worlds, and on the outside would never have run into one another, let alone become friends. But prisons make for strange alliances, and the two got to know and like one another. And they did have one major thing in common, of course. Both had killed the men they loved, men who had betrayed them.

Harris was a sophisticated, intelligent, well-mannered woman who grew up comfortably in conservative Cleveland Heights, Ohio. She was a brilliant and promising student at Smith, where she graduated Phi Beta Kappa and magna cum laude in 1945. A year later, she married James Scholes Harris and became a housewife and mother of two boys, whom she raised in fashionable Grosse Pointe, Michigan. But after nineteen years, Harris yearned for a life and career of her own. It was the mid-1960s, not quite the bra-burning era of the women's liberation movement, but Betty Friedan had already written her watershed book, *The Feminine Mystique*. Women everywhere were realizing that it wasn't just a man's world, that the Pill, coupled with the need for their skills in the marketplace, had empowered them as never before. Jean Harris had reared her children, played hostess, puttered around the house, and taught school long enough in Grosse Pointe. She was ready for her own full-blown career now, and was determined to succeed on her own.

She divorced her husband and took her two boys with her to Philadelphia, accepting a job as administrator at the Springside School.

She worked diligently as a teacher and administrator

and finally attained the position of headmistress of the exclusive Madeira School, in McLean, Virginia.

In 1966 she was introduced to Tarnower, and it was love at first sight. Hy Tarnower was a rough diamond who grew up in Brooklyn, the son of a hatter. He had to scrape by, but his determination, cleverness, and ambition eventually earned him a medical degree, and later made him a household word as his book rode the bestseller lists for years. Not incidentally, he also became a rich man.

Tarnower liked women, but marriage was not a goal of his. Still, he was so taken with Harris that he proposed marriage about two months after they met, then, characteristically, promptly backed out. He had done that before, with other women. Nonetheless, their relationship continued for more than fourteen years, and Harris stayed in love with him all that time. Then she shot him to death on March 10, 1980.

Harris's trial was the East Coast trial of the century. It was to sophisticated New York of 1980–81 what the O.J. case was to star-struck Los Angeles in 1995. It not only involved a famous personality and violent death, it also threw the spotlight on something society was very uncomfortable with, yet had done little to come to grips with: men's abuse—psychological, emotional, and physical—of women.

The killing of Tarnower was such a shocker because it happened at the hands of Jean Harris, a quintessential WASP, a headmistress, a woman of the world, supposedly a model of self-control. Yet she had done the unthinkable. She'd gone out and bought a gun in Virginia, drove to his home in Purchase, in New York's Westchester County, and shot him dead.

Harris maintained all along that she had intended to kill herself, not Tarnower, and had driven to his home to talk to him one more time before committing suicide. Exactly what happened in the bedroom that March night has been the subject of much debate, but Tarnower was shot in the hand and the chest, and died en route to the hospital. And he certainly didn't shoot himself.

The fascination with the case was understandable. People from Harris's world simply did not commit such acts. Harris was a model, not only for the privileged girls who attended Madeira, but for her class. She was a solid citizen, a member of the Establishment, who wouldn't exceed a speed limit, let alone kill a man she had loved for 14 years.

Of course, things are not always as they seem. For Jean Harris, like Vicki Ardito, was also a desperately unhappy woman. Tarnower had tired of her, was seeing other women, and made sure Harris knew about it. She was also under a lot of stress at Madeira, and was feuding with the board of directors. She was overworked. And the depression which had dogged her for years now overwhelmed her. Suicide had entered her thoughts often.

Tarnower, too, was a man who had a side the public didn't see. His self-made fame and fortune, and his charm and apparent sophistication, concealed his frustrations, his insecurities, his complications. He bristled, for example, at never being allowed to forget he was Jewish.

In one of her books, *Stranger in Two Worlds*, Harris describes a conversation she had with Tarnower one evening. She writes:

" 'You know,' he said, 'I'm an agnostic. Now if you were an agnostic, you'd just be an agnostic. But I'm a Jewish agnostic. You never stop being Jewish.' And then, as though he had exposed too much, he laughed and said, 'What the hell. If I hadn't been Jewish it would have been too easy!' I loved that line."

Through Tarnower, Harris, too, was exposed to the not

so subtle forms of anti-Semitism which are the norm in WASP ranks.

"It wasn't until the late 1970s that he was asked to be a member of the Westchester Country Club," she writes.

" 'Now they ask me,' he said, with a rueful smile and some honest bitterness in his voice. 'It would have meant so much to me to be asked 30 years ago. What do I want with the Westchester Country Club today? I was the personal physician of four presidents of that club, but not good enough to be a member.' "

Harris hated to see such discrimination, and sympathized with Tarnower. Liberal headmistress that she was, she couldn't tolerate any prejudice; but Tarnower himself harbored a glaring one: against women.

"Hy was a moral man where his medical practice was concerned," she wrote. "He was amoral where women were concerned. I think he was comfortable with the arrangement because he had divided the world into givers and takers, first class and second class, and men were the former, and women were the latter."

Jean Harris, like Vicki Ardito, was not one to accept being second-class anything.

"He simply never questioned that God designed the sexes to occupy different spheres. He wasn't interested in a woman filling the benign roles of wife and mother. On the other hand, if you worked as hard as he did, and I did, it still didn't buy you more than a second-class ticket to life. His behavior swung from the side of grace to the side of hubris, an anomaly I was never equipped to understand fully or cope with intelligently. Instead, I simply endured it, remembering the good parts, loving enough to forgive the bad parts.

"It would be difficult to describe the nature of our relationship," she writes. "I'm not sure what it was myself, what made him so important to me, what attracted me to him. The forensic psychologist who tested me for more than 19 hours after Hy's death wrote:

'I feel that this patient in the years since 1966 seemed to live what Dr. Memminger would describe as "a partial death and substitute for suicide." She had truncated her life through her subjection to Dr. Tarnower in such a manner as to kill part of herself in masochistic surrender. She had recurring bouts of depression as she realized that she could not free herself from this man . . . who denied her status, sadistically teased her, and was a figure of complicity in her long standing, self-destructive vulnerability.' "

At the time of her trial in 1980, Jean Harris won a lot of support from women's rights activists. They thought Tarnower's death was an accident, or even justifiable homicide.

Harris's version of events leading up to the killing paint her as a weary, disheartened woman—unhappy with Tarnower, yes. But he had been having affairs with other women throughout their relationship. That was no surprise. But she was also unhappy running the Madeira School. She was overworked. She had decided to take her own life.

Harris took the stand at the end of the lengthy trial, and under questioning from her attorney, Joel Aurnou, told a tale that was hard to believe. Indeed, the jury did not believe it at all.

Harris said she surprised Tarnower, who was asleep, and insisted that they talk. He was in no mood. She persisted, became angry, and went into the adjoining bathroom, where she found a blue nightie which presumably belonged to another of his lovers. She threw the nightie on the floor in front of him, then reached for a box of curlers which she hurled across the bathroom, breaking a window. Tarnower, for the first time in his life, slapped her across the face.

Harris then picked up another box, and threw it at a cosmetic mirror, which smashed. Tarnower slapped her again across the face. In the 14 years they had been together, the only thing they had every raised their voices over, she wrote, had been the use of the subjunctive.

Eventually, Harris pulled the gun from her purse, the gun she had bought earlier that day in Virginia. She told Tarnower she was going to kill herself. She then told the court:

"I raised it to my head and pulled the trigger at the instant that Hy came at me and grabbed the gun and pushed my hand away from my head and pushed it down, and I heard the gun explode. It was very loud. . . . Hy jumped back and I jumped back and he held up his hand and it was bleeding and I could see it was bleeding and I could see the bullet hole in it and he said, 'Jesus Christ, look what you did,' and we both just stood there and looked at it. I think he was as appalled as I was. . . ."

Tarnower then went into the bathroom to wash the wound, and Harris retrieved the gun, which had fallen under one of the beds in the room. Returning from the bathroom, Tarnower saw her with the gun again, and dove at Harris, grabbing her left arm. She dropped the gun. Tarnower then retrieved it and buzzed for his household help, a butler and housekeeper, named Henri and Suzanne. Harris pleaded with Tarnower for the return of the gun.

"Hy, please give me the gun, or shoot me yourself, but for Christ's sake, let me die."

Tarnower was now on the phone with one of the servants, and had placed the gun in his lap. Harris reached for it.

"Hy dropped the phone and he grabbed my wrist and

I pulled back and he let go and I went back to the other bed. I fell back the way you would in a tug-of-war and Hy lunged forward at me, as though he was going to tackle me, and his hands came out like that, around my waist, and there was an instant when I felt the muzzle of the gun in my stomach. I thought it was the muzzle of the gun, and I had the gun in my hand and I pulled the trigger and it exploded again, with such a loud sound, and my first thought was: My God, that didn't hurt at all, I should have done that a long time ago. And then Hy fell back. . . ."

Harris got up from the bed, gun still in hand.

"I stopped there at the head of the bed near the closet and I put the gun to my head and I took a very deep breath and I pulled the trigger and the gun clicked."

Joel Aurnou, Harris's defense attorney, asked her, "You mean it fired?"

"No," Harris replied, "it didn't fire. . . . I looked at it and I pulled the trigger and it exploded, I thought . . . [the bullet] had gone possibly into the rug. I found out months later that it had gone into the cupboard right next to the headboard. And I put [the gun] back to my head and I shot and I shot and I shot and I shot and it just clicked. . . ."

The district attorney had a simpler, more logical explanation for how Herman Tarnower was shot—Harris stood over him and pumped several bullets into him. The wound in his hand was explained away as the action of a desperate man trying to defend himself. The bullet that entered his hand, the prosecution maintained, went through it and into his chest.

Harris's story was not what the media, or the public, wanted to believe. It made better copy, and a better story, to believe the prosecution. It was the old story of the rejected woman exacting revenge. And the prosecution had all kinds of evidence to support its claim—evidence which Harris claims was faulty.

The jury didn't believe Harris, who came across as aloof and not at all remorseful. She shed no tears while she told her tale, and juries love tears.

On February 28, 1981, Harris was found guilty of murdering Dr. Herman Tarnower.

Despite the verdict, and the failure of her appeal, there are still many who believe Harris. In *Stranger in Two Worlds*, she makes her case. And is much more convincing as a writer than she was as a witness in her own behalf. She had discovered, to her horror and astonishment, that juries like simple morality plays, not complicated versions of events involving complex people acting in a confused state.

"Part way through the trial an old friend of Hy's, and one he had admired very much for his business acumen, came up to me during a short break. He put his hands on my shoulders and said quietly, 'Jean, you've got to make Hy the bad guy. I've been involved in litigation and I've seen a lot of jury trials. A jury wants a good guy and a bad guy. That's what they can understand. If the bad guy isn't Hy, it will be you. He's gone now. It doesn't matter to him. If you're going to win this trial, you have to make Hy the bad guy.'"

"What happened that night," Harris continued, "could easily have been avoided—by me if I had killed myself on the terrace at Madeira and not indulged myself in the need to see him one more time—by Hy if he had just once understood the depth of my anguish that night and given me ten minutes of his time, or just left me alone to kill myself when I finally tried. There was no way I could bring myself to tell the world I was the good guy and Hy the bad. It would have been easy, but it wouldn't have been true."

On March 20, 1981, Harris was sentenced to prison for 15-years-to-life, which meant no hope of parole for at least 15 years. She was assigned to Bedford Hills Correctional Facility, only a few miles away from the house in Purchase where she shot Tarnower. Three and a half years later, Vicki Ardito joined her there. The urbane Harris and the raucous Ardito had both suffered at the hands of men they loved and had sacrificed for, and both were responsible for their deaths. And now they were inmates in a prison that would be their home for years to come.

As a prison, Bedford Hills is no country club, despite its tony location in one of the most affluent, quiet towns in Westchester. With its spacious, old colonial-era homes, it is an enclave for wealthy executives and professionals who commute to New York City.

But Bedford Hills Prison is no quaint escape. It is as dreary and sad a prison as any found on barren acres in the middle of nowhere. After all, it does house convicted murderers. In fact, in the mid-1980s, 9 percent of the 800 women prisoners were there for murder, and another 23 percent for manslaughter. Harris had an explanation for why there were so many killers, about triple the percentage of previous generations. "Since many of the cases today are the result of domestic violence, one might conclude they are the result of women's new attitude toward themselves, their willingness to stand just so much battering by a man and then no more."

22

Vicki Ardito and Jean Harris had both led very active, absorbing lives and rotting away in prison was the ninth circle of hell for the both of them.

Ironically, as strong-willed as both women were, it would be their physical health that would finally get them beyond the hated walls of Bedford Hills.

Jean Harris would finally be released from prison to undergo a heart operation. But by then, Vicki was already gone.

Her health began to deteriorate right along with her legal hopes. Her attempt to withdraw her guilty plea, based on evidence of Gerald Ardito's supposed involvement, had been denied. Judge Stark's ruling was being appealed. Her thread of hope had become a single strand.

She started coughing a lot, and complained when inmates smoked around her. But despite trips to the hospital infirmary, her condition was not diagnosed until nine weeks later. She turned out to have lung cancer. But again, there was a delay, perhaps a fatal one, in treating her. Six more weeks would pass before she had an operation for the removal of one of her lungs. But it was too late. Cancer had invaded her body's other vital organs.

With just months to live, Vicki and her family and

friends tried to get a medical discharge so she wouldn't have to die in prison.

"I can handle it all, Jean," she told Harris, "except the thought of dying in prison. That's the worst."

Harris, in another of her books, titled *They Always Call Us Ladies*, describes the unusual amount of kindness that other inmates accorded Vicki when her illness became known.

"Maria spends hours with her, gently rubbing her back, talking to her in soothing terms, 'I take care of you, Mommy. You need something, I get for you.' Kathy who lives next door ties a string of yarn between their cells in such a way that Vicki can waken her in the night if she needs help. Ellen cooks her favorite Italian food, and urges her to eat to keep up her strength. Others, returning from the visiting room with packages from home, bring something special to her room—fresh berries, a garden tomato, a new magazine.

"Others with nothing to give come to her room to sit for a little while, sharing the gossip on the floor. It frightens her to be alone, and she is left alone only when we are locked in our cells. Even a few of the most disturbed women try to soothe her pain with kindness."

Even though her days were numbered, Vicki continued her legal fights. She had her attorneys request clemency for her. Governor Mario Cuomo had repeatedly turned down the clemency plea of Jean Harris; he was not about to give clemency to a woman who had confessed to intentional murder.

But in part thanks to Jean Harris, Vicki did obtain release to a hospice, so she did not have to die in prison. Harris had told Burt Schoenbach, an aide to State Senator Israel Ruiz, of Vicki's wish, and of the poor medical care and attention she had received. An investigation was launched by the Health Department's Office of Professional Medical Conduct, and several doctors were questioned. But the damage to Vicki Ardito had already been done.

On August 26, 1987, she was transferred to the Calvary Hospital hospice in the Bronx. Since her cancer had been diagnosed two years before, she had had one lung removed, and part of a second, along with one kidney and her adrenal glands. She wouldn't last long.

On September 14, 1987, Vicki Ardito died.

Harris describes the effect her death had on the inmates.

"Vicki died on a Thursday. She had almost three weeks outside in a hospice, where her children and friends could be with her and she could be a mother and a woman for a while. Sherry and Kelly organized a service for her here at the prison. We held it in the gym because the floor of the chapel is falling in.

"We sat in a semicircle, there were about one hundred of us, and Ceci sang, and a trio sang, and sang, and women went up one at a time and said what was in their hearts about Vicki. Kelly said, 'For those of us who have [had a] hard time like Vicki did, I'll always remember how they came into Vicki's room just before she went out and said to her, "You understand, Miss Ardito, if you get better you've still got to come back and serve nine more years." And Vicki said, "I'll be glad to serve nine more years." '

"Sandy went up too. She's dying of AIDS, but she wanted to say something about Vicki . . . Ceci sang a gospel song by Andrae Crouch:

> Tell them, even if they don't believe you
> Tell them, even if they won't receive you
> Just tell them for me
> Please tell them for me
> That I love them, and I came to let them know.

"A big sign over the prison stage in back of where she stood says, 'We women can make it on our own.' For an hour, Vicki brought out the parts in all of us that make people beautiful."

Even as her illness made her weaker, Vicki had found a way to touch a lot of her fellow inmates. At Christmas time, she asked the 59 women on her floor what they'd like for Christmas. "Then she found pictures of all the things in the magazines," writes Harris, "cut them out and put them in envelopes, with a ribbon, and Christmas afternoon she called them all together and gave each one her gift."

If Vicki Ardito had chosen a gift for herself, it would doubtless have been a picture of bird—one that could have flown, once again, over the cuckoo's nest.

23

Jean Harris lost a friend and a cellmate when Vicki died; she was a woman Harris had learned to care for and understand.

Jed Ardito had lost his mother over a decade earlier, when she was arrested for killing Ben Mattana. From then on, he saw her only briefly, on visits to mental institutions, or during her short absences from South Beach, or at Bedford Hills, or when she was released to die in the hospice.

He never got enough love back from Vicki. Even when she was living at home, before she took off with Mattana, Jed had to share Vicki with his brother and sisters, her grease-monkey friends, and, of course, the real monkeys she kept around.

At the first important milestone in his life, his graduation from Wheatley Heights High, she was in a mental institution. Getting that diploma was a major achievement for Jed, and he would dearly have loved for her to have been at his graduation. But on that big day in 1977, he did have plenty of other company. Bodyguards, hired by his father, attended the graduation ceremonies to ensure his safety—a nice way to start adult life.

It would have been understandable if this troubled young man had turned to drugs, which were readily available all around him, or if he'd taken to drink; but he never did—not then, and not later in life. Perhaps it was because he knew the damage that drugs could do. Cocaine had played a role in his mother's downfall. Scotch made his father a tyrant. His sister Dina was arrested for dealing coke. Like Frank McDarby, Jed had seen close-up the terrible damage that drugs and alcohol can do, especially to people who feel they have the weight of the world on their shoulders.

To his credit, Jed did not try to drown his troubles or run away from them. But he was barely able to cope with them.

In the fall of 1977, he began classes at Fordham University, his father's alma mater. A bad choice. Teachers at Fordham don't take wounded birds under their wing and try to nurture them; it's not that kind of place. Many of the students come from prep schools and Catholic parochial schools in the New York area, and have good reading and writing skills and established study habits.

Jed was lost at Fordham. He was out of his element and couldn't focus. The work was beyond him, and the strain of visiting his mother and trying to study was just too much. He soon dropped out, thereby disappointing his father once again—not that he could have cared much about that.

He had been receiving counseling, of course. But it remained for one counselor, Thomas Bratter, to positively alter the course of Jed's life.

Bratter had a good track record in helping otherwise bright young men in their late adolescence who were having problems realizing their potential.

Bratter took Jed under his wing. It's hard to see how he wouldn't. After all, Jed had a fascinating story to tell, and you had to feel sorry for him—and he did have potential.

Bratter not only lent an intelligent ear to Jed, and helped him deal with his psychological problems, he also helped him get back into college. Jed needed to set out on a course where he could take control of his life, put his past behind him, and have a relatively normal future.

Jed was a lousy student but was nonetheless interested in writing. He had already lived a life worthy of a movie, and he wanted to record it. It was also good therapy. But where could he go, a troubled kid with bad grades? There was a limit to the colleges Jed could attend. The obvious choice turned out to be Sarah Lawrence College, in Bronxville, New York. This small, traditionally women's liberal arts college was not Ivy League, or one of the seven sisters, but it had an enviable reputation as a place where gifted students could really flourish, under the direction of a dedicated and talented teaching staff. At almost any other time in its history, Jed would never have gained admittance.

Due to financial pressure, the school had gone coeducational in 1968, amidst much uproar among the students and alumnae. They thought men would be a distraction and change the very nature of the place. But economic reality could not be denied. As expensive as any Ivy League school, Sarah Lawrence was having trouble attracting enough qualified young women who could afford the high tuition, so like many other all-women schools of the day, it went coed. It was assumed that the move would net the college more qualified applicants to choose from, without lowering standards or tuition.

But men did not flock to Sarah Lawrence, and their numbers were lower than what the administration hoped for. There were plenty of seats for qualified male applicants. By the late seventies, only about 20 percent of the students on campus were male.

And in the school year beginning in fall 1978, there was more room for men than ever. They were staying away in droves.

The reason was a *New York Times* magazine article about the increasing visibility of lesbians on campus. At first, men had thrived at the school—too well. They started to take over, which triggered a fierce backlash among women students, especially the most vocal in their number—including lesbians and women's rights activists. Life for men on the campus changed drastically in the late 1970s. They were considered the enemy by many of the school's women leaders.

In February 1977, a male student named Jim Farber wrote a letter to *The New York Times* describing what life was like for men on the pretty Bronxville campus.

"Being a male at Sarah Lawrence can be a trying experience," he wrote. "Here the oppressed minority are men. . . . Every week it seems a new women's group sprouts with the lesbians and the Marxist feminist collective being the most vocal and longstanding."

Farber complained of sagging admissions standards, and what that had done to the school. "To outsiders who have been given no prior warning, Sarah Lawrence must seem like the only accredited puppy shelter on the Eastern seaboard. Innocently tucked away in conservative Bronxville, the college rarely gives tests, never gives grades (unless you request them), demands no requirements for a major, and offers an almost totally individualized work load. You can even get out of a book review by saying the book isn't 'you.'"

Farber went on to quote the president of the school, Charles DeCarlo, about "unsalable skills" being taught.

"You may get a job as a taxi driver, but at least you'll be a thinking one," said the president.

It was a cheap shot, as Sarah Lawrence has more than its share of illustrious and successful graduates. Its teaching methods might be somewhat unorthodox, but the aim is to graduate students who are independent thinkers.

Farber's letter caused quite a few ripples on campus and among students' parents, but was largely dismissed as the whining of a crank. But a month later, March 20, 1977, *The New York Times* magazine published a cover story by Anne Roiphe, an alumna, entitled "The Trouble with Sarah Lawrence." The piece threw a spotlight on Sarah Lawrence's problems, lending credence to a number of things in Farber's earlier letter. The Sarah Lawrence which Roiphe painted was, indeed, unusual. All you really needed to get in was money. The acceptance rate was an overwhelming 85 percent for all students. Given the desire to increase male enrollments, the admission rate for male applicants was probably even higher. In short, if you were a male high school grad with deep pockets but only a room-temperature IQ, you could probably get into Sarah Lawrence in 1978. Jed Ardito had found himself a college.

While life for students like Jim Farber could be "trying," some male students were having the times of their lives. Despite all the noise about lesbians, most women students were heterosexual, of course. And the straight men on campus were very much in demand. "Everyone around knows if you see an interesting guy on campus he's either got a girl on his arm or a purse on his shoulder," said one coed.

One male student recalls walking across the campus when the weather was warm, hearing women call from their windows to him to come up to their rooms. "It was heaven," he said.

* * *

With plenty of girls around, and no grades, Jed managed to get through Sarah Lawrence. "I remember him as kind of 'Brooklyn,'" says one former classmate. "He was kind of vacuous. He always wanted to get laid."

Jed had indeed found a home. And by the time he graduated, he had achieved what must have earlier seemed impossible to him: he had pulled himself together. Relatively, anyway. It was quite a credit to the teaching staff, which took pains with him. And Jed had already learned to manipulate people who had sympathy for him. Yet graduate he did, and was ready to conquer the world.

The job market that Jed faced in New York City in the early eighties was mixed. Though the Reagan-inspired bull market was well underway, there wasn't a lot of new hiring going on. Jed made the rounds of Manhattan employment agencies, résumé in hand.

Sales appeared a natural for him. He was tall, good looking, had a college degree and a soft, likable manner. His potential struck one employment agency owner, who offered to hire and train Jed himself. So Jed's first job was to get other people jobs.

Among employment agencies, the big action was in placing temporary employees. Large companies were pruning back on their permanent back-office and secretarial help. They preferred hiring temps—who earned no benefits and could be hired and fired at will, as work demands dictated.

The goal for the salesman was to get those corporate accounts. It was no trouble at all finding the temporary workers. In a city like New York, you simply had to run an ad.

He was good at getting accounts, because he soon discovered what it all boiled down to—flattery and entertainment. There was little difference, if any, among temporary-help agencies. They all more or less supplied the same workers. So who got the account? Why not the nice young kid who takes you to lunch?

By wooing the people who pick agencies, Jed did well. But he soon discovered another source of clients: competitors' salespeople; the good ones would take their accounts with them. So Jed monitored and cultivated the competitors' best salespeople, and he'd then hire the best.

With money in his pocket and tasting his first real success, Jed could afford to enjoy the swinging single life in New York City. He did well with women, but he needed something more than just sex. He needed a woman to love, to marry, and share a life with. There had not been a lot of love to go around when he was growing up. He was desperate for it now.

New York has long been the mecca for talented wannabes, who will gladly put up with living in tiny, overpriced apartments and other urban indignities in order to launch their careers. And it has never lacked for plenty of places where like-minded souls of both sexes can mingle. The singles scene is an industry in New York. On any given night, there are dozens of places crammed with singles looking to network, to compare notes, to have a few laughs—and to have sex.

It didn't take long for Jed to find a woman who could give him what he wanted. Her name was Heather Hughes. She was a dancer, and she and Jed fell very much in love and decided to get married. Jed was already doing remarkably well in his new career, and he felt he could afford it.

They talked about where the wedding ceremony should take place, and Jed came up with the perfect suggestion—the grounds of Sarah Lawrence in Bronxville. It seemed only fitting to launch his married life at the same place he had found the first real success.

So it was there, on a bright July day in 1985, that Jed Ardito took his first wife. Only a few miles away, across the county, Vicki Ardito spent that day going about her prison chores at Bedford Hills. Gerald Ardito, his father, was not invited.

24

At first Jed thrived in his marriage, and he did increasingly better in his business. His employer, Eric Goldstein, even backed him and became a co-partner in a temporary-help agency which Jed ran. Jed had definitely found his niche. But if there was some of his mother in Jed—and there was—there was also something of his father. Jed had a roving eye. Like father, like son.

For his wife Heather, the experience of knowing, loving, and marrying Jed proved a painful one. Just as Jed had decided where they would wed—on the campus of his alma mater—he dominated the marriage. He had to have control. And when he got that control, he abused it.

Marie Daniele was 19 and had her teeth in braces when Jed met her and hired her to work for him in 1989. Nonetheless, there was something special about this young, strong, pretty girl. They clicked in a special way.

It didn't make sense for Jed to take up with Marie. For openers, she was his employee. He had hired her away from another temp agency because she had promise, not because she was pretty. Although office romances sometimes do blossom into happy marriages, there is still a lot of truth to the old adage, "Don't fish off the company pier." Especially when you are the boss, and married. Especially in a city like New York, where there are plenty of potential partners running around.

But Jed became fascinated by Marie. She wasn't college educated, but she was smart. She wasn't drop-dead beautiful, but she was pretty and sexy. She was impressed with Jed, and looked up to him.

They flirted, then started dating. While Marie was reluctant to go out with a married man, he assured her his marriage was doomed and divorce was imminent. Seeing each other every day, working closely, then going out afterwards, the relationship would either quickly die of overexposure or take deep root. It flourished. They were very much in love. Jed started divorce proceedings.

On July 20, 1990, Marie's twenty-second birthday, Jed proposed to Marie. It was also his own fifth wedding anniversary.

At first, Marie's family loved this young, successful Sicilian boy, and they welcomed him in like one of their own. Jed felt the warmth of a real old-fashioned Italian family, three generations of Danieles living side by side, in Greenpoint, all involved in each other's lives. Everything revolved around the family. It was a world totally unknown to Jed, who had grown up in a family where the kids were more an annoying afterthought than anything else. Vicki did her thing, Gerald did his, and the kids would have to fend for themselves. Jed grew up spending more time with his mother's boyfriends than with his own father. When he was in his mid-teens, and had lost a few schoolyard scrapes, it wasn't his father who took him out into the backyard to give him a few hints in the manly art of self-defense. It was Benny Ventimiglia, an armed robber and soon-to-be murderer, who drilled him in killer karate.

The Daniele household was one where weekend meals included three generations of the family, and there was as much love as there was pasta around the table. Jed had not known anything like it. The family loved him like the son he was soon to become.

But once accepted into this real family, Jed began to have second thoughts. In the cold, clear light of dawn, was this what he really wanted? He wanted Marie, but did he want her so much that he would be absorbed by her world, her family? Was he doing the right thing?

The marriage wasn't all that imminent—at least another year would have to pass. By both tradition and common sense, Vicki's older sister would go to the altar first. That would allow Jed and Marie time to make sure of their relationship. In the Daniele world, marriage was not something rushed into; it was a lifelong commitment. Marie dreaded that her parents might find out that Jed had already been married, and in fact was still married when he proposed to her.

The delay made sense for the family, too. It gave them time to prepare for another wedding. Jed found that he was in an environment where he could not dictate events. He could not dominate, and he was not in control—Marie and the Danieles were.

With a failed marriage behind him, and another trip down the aisle pending, the last thing that Jed Ardito needed in his life was another woman.

But this was a man who had trouble making commitments, as much as he needed them from others. He needed Marie, and loved and wanted her. But having wooed and won her, there was no more thrill to the chase.

Petra Koss was the first strong temptation that came his way, and Jed could not resist her. She was young, tall, blonde, with a hard, athletic body, an angelic face and skin like alabaster. And she was vulnerable.

It was Petra's bad luck that she exercised at the YMCA pool in midtown Manhattan where Jed also liked to swim in the mornings. Cutting through the water as gracefully as a mermaid, lots of men's eyes followed her. But Jed could not simply admire her and walk away. Here was a challenge he could not resist. When she climbed out of the pool, he started a conversation with her.

To his delight, he found that she was not a hard-boiled New York career girl, used to fending off advances from strangers. She was a stranger in town herself, from Austria, and as innocent as she was beautiful. She was twenty-four years old, unattached, and staying temporarily in New York working for the Austrian delegation.

Jed quickly discovered that the soft-spoken and polite Petra was well-educated, from a wealthy family, fluent in several languages, a skilled horsewoman and skier. He couldn't believe his luck—or turn down the temptation.

He took her for a walk after meeting her at the pool, something of a conquest in itself. But his flirtation didn't stop there. Thoughts of Marie, if he had any at all, failed to deter him.

Petra found Jed charming, and agreed to see him again. And again. She was then unaware of Jed's involvement with Marie, and enjoyed being with him. Until she met him, New York had been almost like a prison.

Jed saw more and more of her, showing her the city she had longed to explore, but was afraid to see on her own. She was dazzled by this dark, sophisticated man, who filled an aching void in her life. "He had a way of making a woman feel like a woman," she said. "I was very insecure and didn't know who I was."

For as dazzling as Petra was in appearance, she was a flawed jewel. Her parents had divorced when she was young, and that had badly scarred her. She lacked confidence, and had low self-esteem. She had become bulimic, which frightened and depressed her. She knew how dangerous that could be.

But Jed changed all that. He was as exotic and exciting to her as she was to him. He was confident with her, and gave her security. He showed her off to his friends and associates, and they made her feel even more comfortable.

Petra was falling very much in love. She no longer felt the need to vomit her meals, and overcame her bulimia. She'd been swept off her feet, and loved every moment of it.

But Petra's growing happiness and confidence were mirrored by Marie Daniele's hurt and despair. Jed had taken over Marie's life, become part of her family, and promised to love her for the rest of his life. Yet within months he had dropped her like a stone for some Austrian pastry.

The engagement was broken; Marie was simply discarded. Her pain was only compounded by having to see Jed every day at work, knowing that he had been with Petra the evening before, knowing that he would be with her again that evening. She heard the men in the office go on and on about Petra. They called her a perfect 10 and envied Jed his good fortune. Marie was shattered. She couldn't believe what was happening. Nor could her family. What kind of man was this, to take up with another woman so soon after proposing to Marie? He got engaged to Marie in July, and started seeing Petra in October.

Yet even as the whirlwind romance became more serious, and Jed and Petra spoke of marriage, Marie knew there was something very wrong with this picture. She knew Jed as no one else did. She knew that Petra would be in for a shock. There was no doubt in her mind that they were all wrong for one another. But that was small consolation when she heard that Jed and Petra were, indeed, going off to Austria to get married. It was the second time in six months he had made a proposal of marriage. He would follow through with this one.

It would have been Jed and Marie's first Christmas together as an engaged couple. It would have been a time of great celebration in the family, a time for planning, a time of love. Instead, her Jed had abandoned her and her family, and settled for a trophy Marie knew was only gold-plated.

There was a quiet, civil wedding in Austria in December, followed by a fairy-tale ceremony in January 1991, that took place in a picture-book Alpine church. Petra wore a splendid, jeweled tiara which had been in her family for generations. Her family was delighted at the nuptials. Petra's father had taken a strong liking to his new Italian-American son-in-law, and felt confident that Jed would take care of his adorable, but troubled, daughter.

There was fancy balls, and rides on horseback in the Austrian countryside, and wonderful moments together for the newlyweds. But the fairy tale would not last long.

Back in New York City, Jed no longer played the role of the handsome, strong protector. He began to tell Petra of his past. Things about his mother. Things about Marie.

Petra was bewildered. Just as Jed had changed soon after becoming engaged to Marie, he became a different man once he married Petra. She wanted to rely on him; instead Jed unloaded a host of frightening problems on her, which she was unable to fathom. Her prince turned into a frog.

"I felt like I was Jed's social worker, or counsellor," she said.

Thoughts of his mother haunted him. For the first time, Jed told Petra the whole truth about her; before then, he had only said she had spent a lot of time in psychiatric hospitals. He had never told her why. It was only after the the marriage that Petra discovered she had married the son of a killer.

"He said that if he could love me, he would have to kill his mother in his mind," Petra said. "He loved his mother very much, and he hated her also."

Jed told her stories about Vicki, which she found very chilling. He had even had to fight with chimpanzees "because they were jealous of Jed's relationship with his mother."

Petra also discovered that Jed couldn't stand to be alone. "He used to say, 'when I am by myself the devils are coming. I am not rational like you are. I am sometimes irrational. When I am by myself, I see red in my head.' "

Worst of all, Petra found out Marie was still very much in his heart and mind. He talked about her all the time, about how she had hurt him. "I believed the stories that he told me, that Marie was demanding of him," said Petra. "When he was lying, he was a very good liar. He believed 100 percent what he was lying about."

Petra met Marie, and found her quite different. "She was like a very normal woman," she said. And she also noticed something else about Marie which Jed had never mentioned. "She was very similar to his mother."

Jed talked incessantly about Marie. "There was something between him and Marie that he could not break, something very fatal. He was desperate and couldn't get away from her."

She learned that Jed was seeing Marie again—and had started to do so within days of their wedding. No wonder the magic had gone out of their marriage bed so quickly. And her bulimia had returned.

But Petra tried to convince herself that she could still save their marriage, that Jed would eventually get over Marie. Petra still loved him very much. But he kept on talking about her, and about how mean she was to him. He would get angry, and Petra began to fear him. "There were occasions when I was afraid, really afraid." Then, one day, he said something that frightened Petra so much she had to leave him.

"He said, 'Marie was so mean to me I fear that one day I will kill her and then you will be the one to come to visit me in prison like I did my mother,' " Petra recalled.

Stunned and frightened, Petra immediately left Jed and moved into a separate apartment. As much as she loved him, how could she live with someone so troubled? But the marriage was so fresh—how could she go home so quickly?

But one day not long afterwards, Jed called her and promised things would be different. "Petra, I really love you and want you to come back to me and I will end my relationship with Marie."

The new bride decided to give her new husband another chance.

"I had a good feeling for a few days," she said.

It didn't last. It was clear to Petra that Jed could not rid his thoughts of Marie. Yet one night after dinner, when Petra said she would have to leave him, Jed pleaded with her to stay, because he could not bear to be alone.

Desperate, confused, yet still wanting to help Jed, Petra suggested that he should talk to his ex-wife Heather, perhaps return to her.

Jed called her, and had Petra listen in on the telephone extension. "A half-hour conversation made her a wreck," Petra said. "She was crying. 'Jed, please stop,' she said. 'I don't want to see you any more.'

"He wanted to show me what power he had over Heather."

That was the last straw. Petra told Jed that she had tried hard to work on their marriage but she was going back to her parents in Austria. "He stood up with a crazy look in his eyes. 'I think I should leave the apartment,' he said. 'You are as mean as the other woman.'"

Petra packed her bags for Vienna, and left within hours. She was thirty pounds lighter than her normal weight. Upon arrival, she checked into a hospital for treatment of her bulimia, and stayed two months. And then she tried to put Jed and the whole horror of a bad marriage out of her head.

She would not hear again from Jed, or about him, for two years—when she learned he had strangled Marie in the Grand Hyatt Hotel. She said she was not all that surprised: "I knew that he would kill her."

The relationship between Jed and Marie would always be strained by his having broken their engagement and married Petra. No matter how strongly Marie felt for Jed, she knew that he was capable of hurting her as no one else ever had, or probably could. She had been totally committed to him, and he had broken her heart and insulted her family. She could never really trust him again.

At least she didn't have to see him every day. Jed was responsible for that. When he went off to Austria for the fairy-tale wedding, Eric Goldstein had fired her. Goldstein didn't want any friction in the office when Jed returned. Marie promptly got another job at a competing agency, however, and continued on with her career.

Jed, on the other hand, was not quite as able to return to a status quo after Petra. He was in financial difficulty. After all, he'd gone through two divorces in less than a year. He ended the partnership with Goldstein and started a photo agency for models. He even hired one of Marie's sisters, but it was not a success. Whether the enterprise had been intended to make him a fortune or give him the opportunity to meet a bevy of beautiful young women didn't matter. It did neither.

The relationship was already doomed, but Jed and Marie continued to see one another for about two years after Petra left. It was a roller-coaster ride. By that time, they had become skilled at hitting one another's hot buttons. She would flirt, sometimes have a cocktail too many, leave messages on his answering machine. He would see other women, pretend she meant nothing to him—and also leave messages for her. In an age of beepers, answering machines, and cellular phones, they were in constant communication.

Physically, however, nothing had changed—at least not for Jed. Marie could satisfy him as no other woman could. And he could not get her out of his system. Marie, finally, decided she could and she would. Prodded by friends and her sisters, she decided she would have to end it all and get on with her life.

The night of February 18, 1993, should have been the last time Marie ever saw Jed. That Sunday evening, when Marie was shaking with fear in the apartment of a stranger in Jed's building, she should have realized how dangerous the situation had become. Jed had just tried to choke her. There were marks on her neck from his hands. And Jed might have continued had not a neighbor, alerted by her screams, come to his apartment door and chased Jed away with a baseball bat.

As Jed scampered over fences and down back alleys to avoid a confrontation with police, who were en route to the building, Marie should have let him continue on running, right out of her life. When the police, responding to the neighbor's 911 call, asked her if she wanted to have Jed arrested, she should have said yes. When her brother-in-law, Steve Cairo told her in the car on the way home never to go near him again, she should have taken it to heart.

But she did not. "The problem in so many of these cases is the women are intimidated and embarrassed," said Linda Fairstein, head of the Manhattan district attorney's sex crimes and domestic violence unit. "They see the man they once loved, they see the man they loved and slept with, not some mug shot. They don't realize than an abuser is a criminal." And sometimes a killer.

25

A murder trial is like a war, with long periods of tedium interrupted by decisive moments of battle. But the combatants are lawyers, who are not fighting for their own lives; money and reputation, yes, but it is the defendant in a murder trial whose life, or a major part of it, is the issue.

At stake in *The People* vs. *Gerald Victor Ardito* was the better part of Jed Ardito's adult life. The state sought a conviction for murder in the second degree, which in New York State calls for a sentence of 25 years to life. Found guilty, that would mean that the 35-year-old Ardito would likely be imprisoned until age 60, or the year 2018.

Ardito's defense was that the death of Marie Daniele was an accident, that he had no intention of killing her. But even if the jury believed him, he would still have to face lesser charges. For there was no question he was responsible for her death, and he did not deny that. He could be found guilty of first-degree manslaughter, which in New York State calls for a sentence not to exceed 25 years; or to second-degree manslaughter, calling for up to 15 years.

Or, the jury might find him guilty of the lightest charge of all, criminally negligent homicide, which calls for up to 4 years. That would mean freedom for Ardito in, at most 2½ years, considering his time served.

To the families of murder victims, there is irony in the term "criminal justice." It seems that the whole point of a trial is to ensure that the rights of the accused are preserved at all cost; the defendant has a lot more rights than the mute, dead, absent victim. It's often said that in a murder case the first person put on trial is the victim. Especially in cases involving sex, and a beautiful young woman. The defense tries to plant in the minds of jurors that the dead victim must have done something to encourage, or even somehow deserve, what happened. Make the victim out to be the bad guy, and the accused the good guy.

As attorneys joust over fine points of the law, with the judge acting as referee, the family of the victim sits in bafflement wondering what is happening to the plain, unvarnished truth. The loved ones of murder victims have a hard time accepting that the rules of the game are more important than their idea of justice being served.

Writer Dominick Dunne has written brilliantly about the celebrated murder trials of Claus von Bulow and the Menendez brothers. Most recently, he was accorded celebrity-writer status and a ringside seat at the O.J. Simpson trial, which he was covering for *Vanity Fair*. Dunne was also a commentator on the trial for CBS.

He certainly earned that status. For Dunne is not only a fine and perceptive writer, he also has special insight, drawn from personal experience. He could tell what the families of Nicole Brown and Ronald Goldman were going through, and he would be able to empathize with the family of Marie Daniele, because he had experienced the same tragic loss. He, too, had lost a beautiful young daughter, who was strangled to death by her ex-boyfriend. He, too, had suffered through a torturous murder trial.

And he, too, was mystified, outraged, and saddened at what went on.

What happened to Dominique Dunne on October 30, 1982, at the age of 23, had eerie parallels to what happened to Marie Daniele. Her story is worth retelling.

Dominique Dunne was beautiful, talented, and ambitious, and was already a film star at the time of her death on October 30, 1982. Among her credits, she had played a memorable role in the film *Poltergeist*. If you saw the film, you'll remember her screaming the line, "What's happening?" when weird things start to take place in her home. She also had acted in a number of television shows.

Dominique had an ex-boyfriend, John Sweeney, who was a chef at the trendy Ma Maison restaurant in Los Angeles. The couple had lived together for a while, but Dominique had ended the relationship. "He's not in love with me," she explained to her father, who didn't like Sweeney anyhow, and was glad to see the relationship end. "He's obsessed with me," she said. "It's driving me crazy."

But Dominique had neglected to tell her father that Sweeney had assaulted her and choked her on the very night she ended the relationship. That event took place five weeks before her killing. Nor did Dominique tell him that she had been beaten by Sweeney on two other prior occasions.

Dunne later discovered that Sweeney had a history of abusing women. He had severely beaten another woman he had been involved with, had beaten her on at least ten separate occasions, in fact, over a two-year period. The woman, Lillian Pierce, had been hospitalized twice as a result of those beatings, once for six days, the other for four. Sweeney had broken her nose, punctured her eardrum, collapsed her lung, and thrown rocks at her.

In writing about his daughter and the trial in his book

Fatal Charms, Dunne recalled sitting at his former wife's home, a few nights after Dominique's funeral, when an episode of *Hill Street Blues* came on. Dominique was featured in it, and the program was dedicated to her memory. Her role was that of a battered child. "What we would not know until the trial," wrote Dunne, "was that the marks on her neck were real, from John Sweeney's assault on her five weeks before he killed her."

After that assault, Dominique made no secret of the fact that she was terrified of Sweeney. She told her agent, fellow actors, and friends about the beating, and how afraid she was.

During Sweeney's trial, a hearing was held to determine if evidence of Sweeney's abuse of women would be admitted. With the jury out of the courtroom, Lillian Pierce, his former girlfriend, testified under oath about the batterings she suffered from Sweeney.

A very curious thing occurred during the cross-examination of Pierce. The Assistant District Attorney asked Pierce, "Do you come from a well-to-do family?" The defense objected.

"I am trying to establish a pattern," explained the ADA.

With that, Sweeney exploded from his defendant's chair and bolted for the rear door of the courtroom, and had to be wrestled to the ground and returned to his chair in handcuffs.

"It was an explosion of anger," wrote Dunne. "It showed us how little it took to incite John Sweeney to active rage. Like most of the telling moments of the trial, however, it was not witnessed by the jury."

Then Dominique's mother, Lenny, took the stand and described Dominique coming to her house one evening after one of the beatings she received at the hands of Sweeney—the first of three. Sweeney had bashed Dominique's head on the floor and pulled clumps of hair out of her head.

But Judge Burton S. Katz ruled that the prosecution could not use the testimony of Lillian Pierce, which would have shown a pattern of violence and abuse. He ruled that "the prejudicial effect of the testimony outweighed its probative value."

Nor could the testimony of Dominique's mother be used in the main case, nor statements made by Dominique to her friends and agent about the beatings and her fear of Sweeney during the final five weeks of her life. The judge said that was only hearsay, and was inadmissible as evidence.

Dunne was beginning to get the feeling that the deck was heavily stacked against the prosecution. He took some encouragement, however, from the opening argument in the case, delivered by Assistant District Attorney Steven Barshop.

"He began with a description of the participants. Sweeney: 27, six-foot-one, 170 pounds. Dominique: 22, five-foot-one, 112 pounds," wrote Dunne.

"He described how Sweeney had walked out of Ma Maison restaurant at 8:30 that evening [October 30, 1982] and proceeded on foot to the house, where he argued with Dominique and strangled her. He said that Dominique was brain dead there at the scene of the strangulation, despite the fact that she was kept on the life-support system at Cedars-Sinai Hospital until November 4. He said the coroner would testify that death by strangulation took between four and six minutes. Then he held up a watch with a second hand and said to the jury, 'Ladies and gentlemen, I am going to show you how long it took for Dominique Dunne to die.' For four minutes, the courtroom sat in hushed silence. It was horrifying. I had never allowed myself to think how long she had struggled in his hands, thrashing for her life. A gunshot or a knife stab is over in an instant; a strangulation is an eternity. The only sound during the four minutes came from Michael Adelson [the defense attorney] and John Sweeney, who whispered together the whole time."

The defense had its work cut out for it, but got a break. Sweeney's history of prior abuse of women was not admitted. The defense therefore made it seem as if Dominique had somehow contributed to her own death— blame the victim, make the accused a good guy—and that she had died accidentally.

Sweeney himself took the stand. "He was abjectly courteous," wrote Dunne, "addressing the lawyers and judges as sir. He spoke very quietly, and often had to be told to raise his voice so the jury could hear. Although he wept, he never once became flustered. . . . He painted his relationship with Dominique as nearly idyllic. He gave the names of all her animals—the bunny, the kitten, the puppy. He refuted the testimony of other witnesses and denied that he had tried to choke Dominique after their night on the town five weeks before the killing. He said he'd only tried to restrain her from leaving the house. He admitted that they had separated after that, and that she had had the locks changed so he could not get back in the house, but he insisted that she had promised to reconcile with him and that her refusal to do so was what brought on the final attack. He could not, he claimed, remember the events of the murder. . . ."

Sweeney had blamed the victim. And it worked. In the end the jury ruled that Sweeney was guilty, not of murder in the second degree but of voluntary manslaughter; the earlier choking attack was ruled a misdemeanor.

"There was a gasp of disbelief in the courtroom," wrote Dunne. "The maximum sentence for the two charges is six and a half years, and with good time and work time, the convict is paroled automatically when he has served half his sentence, without having to go through a parole hearing. Since the time spent in jail between the arrest and the sentencing counted as time served, Sweeney would be free in two and a half years."

No one can say for certain how the jury would have found had the testimony of Lillian Pierce and Dominique's mother been allowed in evidence. But such a pattern of violent behavior certainly would have made it much easier for the jury to believe that Sweeney had deliberately killed Dominique, and they may have found him guilty of murder in the second degree.

Jed Ardito was charged with the identical crime as John Sweeney. But even before his trial could begin, the judge in Ardito's case would have to rule on the admissibility of evidence of Ardito's prior attempt to choke Marie Daniele, on February 18, 1993. If it was allowed in, it would help support the prosecution's contention that Ardito had deliberately murdered Marie Daniele. It would indicate that he had choked her before, not in a hotel room, not with suggestions that sex was involved, but in the lobby of his apartment building.

So before the trial of Jed Ardito could get underway, a hearing had to be held on whether the events of that evening, and the 911 tapes on which Marie could actually be heard screaming frantically could be admitted. If they were, the prosecution would have a much stronger case. It was called a Ventimiglia hearing.

26

In agreeing to take on the Ardito defense case, Detective Frank McDarby had not only to suspend judgment on Jed Ardito. He had to give him the benefit of any doubt.

In working with him in building his defense, he visited Ardito often at Rikers Island, and later at the Brooklyn Men's Correctional Center, where he was transferred. It was not an easy time at Rikers—it never is.

He had become a Muslim, taking the name Oomar Shribe Islam, and wore white robes and a black skullcap. As Dominick Dunne wryly observed about his daughter's murderer, who had also suddenly become devout and carried a Bible with him to court every day during his trial, "It is the fashion among the criminal fraternity to find God."

But Ardito was serious enough about his new faith to even wear his Muslim attire into court. McDarby and Ardito's lawyers cringed at this and urged Jed to wear a suit into court. Judges and juries look askance at instant conversions, especially of white defendants to a predominantly black religion. Reluctantly, Jed agreed. But he still insisted on following the tenets of the faith, and that meant there could be no court proceedings on Fridays, the Muslim holy day. To New York judges, who are under great pressure to clear their calendars, losing one day a week because of a defendant's new religion does not score points.

McDarby would not learn until after the trial that Ardito had originally tried a different defense—that he was mentally incompetent. Like mother, like son. But prison psychiatrists wouldn't buy it. There was no question that Ardito had emotional problems, but an insanity defense would just not wash.

McDarby visited Ardito often, corresponded with him, and got to like him. Ardito certainly had had a lot of tough breaks, but he was personable, and certainly a lot different from any of the other killers McDarby had come in contact with when he was a detective.

When McDarby knocked on doors, he almost didn't have to be asked for identification. He had detective written all over him—one from the old school. He had the build of a retired linebacker and a face you could plot Ireland on. His voice and manner had been conditioned by years of trying to make himself indifferent. But there was a look in his eye that made you take him seriously. He was extremely good with his thick hands. And looked to be.

But off the job he was a pussycat. When St. Francis of Assisi Church at 135 East 31st Street in Manhattan had a theft problem, the pastor called McDarby, an old friend. It was near Easter, a season as important to churches as it is to retailers. Someone was systematically ripping off the poor box at the church. With its location in midtown Manhattan, lots of Catholic office workers would drop in, especially around Easter, make a visit, and leave something in the poor box. It was that or drop it in the outstretched hands of the homeless on the church steps.

McDarby was asked to nab the thief. There was only one way to do it, and it wasn't very scientific. He had to hide out in the church all night and wait for the perpetrator.

McDarby hid himself carefully in the shadows and waited, and waited. Finally, a shabbily dressed man appeared at the poor box and began jimmying it open. McDarby sprang from the shadows and leapt upon the man, who was wise enough not to resist but just fell to the floor in astonishment. Looking up at McDarby, he said, "My God, they had to send a detective to get me?" McDarby had never laid eyes on the man before. There was no way he could have known he was a detective.

If people were at home when McDarby knocked on the door, and they looked through the peepholes first to see who it was, they did one of two things. They immediately opened the door if they weren't guilty of anything, or they ran like hell if they were.

In the course of gathering information and evidence to help Jed's case, McDarby interviewed dozens of people. One of the missions McDarby had was to establish that Jed had seen Marie on numerous occasions after February 18, 1993, the night of the so-called 911 incident in the lobby of Jed's building. That would weaken the prosecution's contention that he had lured her up to the hotel room in the Grand Hyatt to attempt a reconciliation, and when that ploy failed, he had strangled her to death because he was unwilling to accept the rejection.

The most important immediate problem the defense faced, however, was the Ventimiglia hearing, to determine the admissibility of the 911 tapes and other evidence from the night of February 18, 1993, when Jed and Marie fought in the lobby of his apartment building at 336 West 49th Street.

Jed's attorneys naturally did not want the 911 tapes from that evening to be used in court. If the prosecution was able to argue in the course of the trial that Jed had choked Marie before, his rough-sex defense would be severely weakened. It would be a lot harder to convince a jury that he had killed her accidentally, in the throes of passionate, kinky sex, if he had choked her only a few weeks before in his apartment lobby.

There were witnesses to that event, the defense knew, who had seen and participated in what had happened that night. Neighbors were awakened by the commotion, and had called 911, threatened Jed with a baseball bat, and had taken Marie into their apartment. And they would doubtless testify for the prosecution.

McDarby went to see if any of the other tenants in the building could remember that night. Maybe they would remember things differently and testify for the defense.

It was a warm June day, and as McDarby walked along West 49th Street, he was thinking of how in a few weeks he'd be going to Ireland again. He'd been going to Ireland at the end of each summer now for eight or nine years in a row—bringing kids both Protestant and Catholic back to Belfast who had spent the summer with families in the U.S. It was a program that aimed to expose kids from war-torn Belfast to a different world where religion didn't matter and where British soldiers didn't rule the streets.

McDarby had been involved in the program almost from its inception. He still had that much Irish in him, three generations removed.

The apartment building where the 911 incident took place was an old brownstone, six stories high, with no elevator. It took a lot of knocking, and several trips at different hours, before McDarby did turn up a key defense witness. A woman who lived on the ground floor said she remembered hearing a couple arguing in the lobby that night. The noise had woken her up. And she heard a woman screaming "He's trying to choke me!"

But the tenant didn't take it seriously because, she said, the girl sounded drunk. It certainly didn't sound serious enough for her to call the police.

McDarby took down her name and number and thanked her very much. He'd found what the defense lawyers were looking for.

27

When Jed Ardito was first arrested and charged with the murder of Marie Daniele in April of 1993, there was a flurry of media interest in the case. On the surface, it resembled another famous New York murder case involving a young man named Robert Chambers. The "preppie killer," as the media dubbed him, had killed Jennifer Levin, a young college student, in Central Park.

Chambers claimed that he had been engaging in "rough sex," and that Levin's death had been accidental. His defense outraged many citizens, not only womens' groups. It seemed preposterous, especially since Levin had suffered marks, bruises, and scratches on her face and body. The Chambers trial was covered gavel to gavel by the national media, and won a lot of viewers and sold a lot of newspapers, books, and magazines.

It was the first nationally publicized use of the rough-sex defense. To the man in the street, such a defense made about as much sense as the "orphan" defense— someone kills his parents, then asks for leniency because he has no parents. It was hard for the layman to take seriously, since rough sex is hardly a common practice among average citizens.

As it turned out, after a lengthy trial, while the jury was deliberating, Chambers finally agreed to a plea. He pled guilty to manslaughter in the first degree, but with a sentence customary for second-degree manslaughter—five to fifteen years. The district attorney had sought a conviction for murder.

The public was outraged at the deal Chambers got—and that outrage sold a lot more newspapers and got a lot more TV ratings.

Jed Ardito was another Robert Chambers in the eyes of the media, but a bit older, and somewhat more successful. *New York Newsday* called him "a $150,000 a year sales representative who wore a Cartier watch, Hermès shirts and showered his girlfriend with expensive jewelry." And his victim, so young and so pretty, completed the picture.

The case originally got plenty of attention. When the crime was committed, when Ardito was arrested, and at his bail hearing, the media covered it extensively.

It was over a year after Marie's death that the first important element of Jed Ardito's trial came before the courts—the pretrial hearing on the 911 call. The hearing took place in July 1994, only a few weeks after O.J. Simpson had been charged with slaughtering his ex-wife and Ron Goldman. And there had been plenty of evidence of prior abuse of Nicole Brown Simpson by O.J. There was even a dramatic 911 call, after one battering finally had O.J. locked up.

Women's groups again took up arms over the repeated failure of authorities to handle women-abusers. Had the authorities taken matters seriously enough when the police were called in the first place, Nicole would still be alive, they argued. And so would many other women, whose husbands or boyfriends had wound up killing them after histories of physical abuse.

Jed Ardito had previously abused Marie Daniele, and

there was a 911 call and witnesses to prove it. Shades of the O.J. case. Why should they even have to hold a hearing on such evidence, the womens' groups asked.

But legally it was a very touchy matter. It was powerful evidence against Jed. If he was convicted, and it could be demonstrated that the judge erred in his judgment in admitting that evidence, a higher court would overturn the verdict. There would have to be a new trial.

The man in the spotlight was State Supreme Court Judge Franklin Weissberg. In court, Weissberg has the personality of broken glass. You deal with him very, very carefully and even then you are probably going to get nicked anyway. His sharp tongue is always ready to strike, and does so frequently. Lawyers approach him the same way porcupines make love—very carefully.

On July 14, 1994, Weissberg concluded the hearing on the 911 tapes. The media was there in force.

In its "Affirmation in Support of the Ventimiglia Motion," Assistant District Attorney Harvey D. Rosen made the people's case concise, clear, and powerful.

It cited the witnesses, who "indicated they heard a woman later identified as Marie Daniele, screaming in the hallway of 336 West 49th Street—Don't hurt me! Somebody help."

The report went on: "A man subsequently identified as Jed Ardito was observed by at least one of the witnesses with his hands around the throat of Marie Daniele. . . .

"Eventually the witnesses to the assault by this defendant got Ms. Daniele inside their apartment and in a highly emotional and traumatized state Ms. Daniele attempted to tell the 911 operator what had transpired. According to police reports some of the witnesses to this incident observed reddish marks on the throat of Ms. Daniele. Ms. Daniele indicated the defendant was trying to kill her."

It then went on to address Ardito's defense: ". . . the

defendant will claim that this was 'rough sex.' That on a number of occasions the defendant claims that he and the deceased, as part of their 'sexual practices' engaged in 'erotic asphyxia,' a method of heightening the orgasm of the deceased.

"In essence the defendant is claiming his manual strangulation of the deceased on April 28, 1993, was an accident. It is the People's contention that this was no accident but an intentional or reckless depraved act of Murder. Admission into evidence of the prior uncharged assault of February 18, 1993, is highly relevant and probative in disproving that the defendant's acts of April 28, 1993, were an accident . . . but a deliberate attempt to take her life."

Rosen had put the judge over a barrel. If the tapes were out, Ardito's rough-sex defense would be a lot stronger. On the other hand, if the tapes were in, the prosecution's case got stronger. It was prior evidence of him assaulting her. But how would a higher court rule on appeal?

The attorneys for Jed's defense tried to pooh-pooh what happened the night of February 18, 1993. They maintained that it was a lover's spat, that the pair had been out late drinking, and no real harm was intended. As part of their argument, they cited the neighbor whom Frank McDarby had interviewed. "They sounded like they had been drinking," she said.

The defense also maintained that since Marie filed no charges against him, and continued to see him after that incident, she didn't take the threat seriously. McDarby had gathered evidence supporting Jed's claim that she had continued to see him after February 18.

Justice Weissberg bit the bullet and charged headlong into a media gauntlet when he declared the 911 tapes inadmissible. He found them "ambiguous," and "did not believe the defendant intended to murder her."

His ruling went on: "The 911 tape clearly reveals the

deceased was hysterical and fearful. However, there is no indication from the tape that she believed the defendant was trying to kill her. . . .

"While battered women frequently refuse to file complaints against abusers, the fact that Ms. Daniele soon after resumed her relationship with the defendant is strong evidence that she did not believe he intended to murder her."

The media had heard the tapes with their own ears in the courtroom and couldn't understand the judge's ruling. Andrea Peyser, a star columnist for the *New York Post*, went for Weissberg's jugular.

In her column of July 19, 1994, she wrote: "If O.J. Simpson faced trial in New York, he would barely need a defense at all. Because some zany and brainless judge likely would do all the work to get him off the hook. And for free.

"A case in point is Justice Franklin Weissberg . . . Remember the name, because it's the guy you want presiding over your trial if you happen to be a guy who killed the woman you claim to love."

This would not be an easy trial for anyone. Not for the judge, who was now in the spotlight as a sexist. Not for the prosecution, which had lost its best evidence of prior abuse. The tapes were chilling—a voice from the grave, crying for help. But they were out.

The defense would not have such an easy time, either. The problem was: how to introduce the rough-sex defense. The only witness they could call to the stand to support it was Jed. Putting a murder defendant on the stand is always risky. The jury might judge him a "bad guy," as had happened with Jean Harris, for example. Or the prosecution might seize on something he says, and destroy him in cross-examination. It promised to be quite a trial.

28

On November 1, 1994 a little over a year and a half after Marie Daniele was killed, the main trial finally got underway.

It was held in Room 1302, in the New York State Supreme Court Building at 100 Centre Street in lower Manhattan.

The building was meant to impress when it was built. From the street, you must walk up a long flight of stone steps before entering a massive lobby with only darkness for a ceiling. Walking into the building should fill one with awe and respect. This is the power of the state, rendered in granite and marble—permanent, solid, definitive.

But today one does not simply stroll into that courthouse—or any of the three major courthouses clustered around Foley Square—city, state, and federal—not after a rash of shootings in courthouses around the country in the early nineties. Snaking out of the building's two entrances are long lines of people waiting to be searched and scanned, a tedious ordeal undergone by all visitors to the building—defendants on bail showing up for hearings or trials, witnesses, their relatives and friends, spectators, prospective and sitting jurors.

The searches are taken seriously, and there is good reason for that. In the bushes outside the building, security people routinely find guns and knives stashed. Visitors undergo yet another search before entering the courtrooms. This neoclassic monolith of a building no longer impresses, rather, it instills fear. The state gets respect one way or the other.

Most of the people waiting on line—the wait can be 20 minutes at the peak morning period—don't seem to mind. They are people used to lines—they are not the elite of New York.

Security guards do manage to confiscate some weapons—small knives, usually, oversights on the part of their owners. More often, they find drugs.

The cavernous lobby buzzes, especially on Monday mornings, which are especially busy. The newspaper stand and the cafeteria do a brisk business dispensing coffee and fast food. Visitors scan lists to see which courtroom to go to. Lawyers cruise to pick up their clients. Reporters scan the calendar and try to determine which trial or hearing has the best potential for a byline.

It is not hard to spot the families of victims of violent crimes, who come to attend trials. They huddle together, talking in whispers, hopeful of vengeance.

The Daniele family was always present in the courtroom in strength. The sons and sons-in-law, big strapping young men, would occasionally stare at the back of Jed Ardito's head, boring holes through it. How could this clean-cut man, who looked more like a lawyer than a defendant, have done such a thing to their precious Marie? But they didn't dwell on the why—they knew what he did, and they wanted the courts to mete out the maximum punishment. They knew their presence might help sway a jury to that decision, and so they came. They knew what they would hear might be painful. They felt most for Marie's mother Angie, who would have to hear gory details of her daughter's death, and see pictures of her lifeless and grotesquely swollen face.

Worst of all, they knew, she would likely hear Jed, her would-have-been son-in-law, describe in minute detail the kinky sexual practices he said Marie and he engaged in. And how in the midst of sexual intercourse, Jed had accidentally killed her. When Jed took the stand to tell his own story, as he was scheduled to do, Angie Daniele and her whole family would have to relive Marie's death all over again.

The jurors and alternates were mostly women, mostly middle-aged or older, mostly black or Hispanic, hardly unusual for a Manhattan criminal court.

Judge Weissberg runs a tight ship, and he made it clear from the trial's outset that he wouldn't tolerate tardiness from the jurors or frivolous motions or objections from the attorneys.

Years on the bench had taught him that there was no advantage in acting friendly toward anyone but the jurors. He was strictly business with everyone else and tolerated no nonsense.

With the O.J. hearing dominating public attention, comparisons with Judge Lance Ito were inevitable. Andrea Peyser, in her *New York Post* column, had lambasted Weissberg for being on the side of the defendant, for knocking out the 911 tapes.

But Weissberg was no Ito, whose mild manner had brought him widespread criticism, mainly for letting the lawyers take control of the courtroom, and causing endless delays that eventually frayed the nerves of the jury to the point of mutiny.

But Weissberg and Ito are like chalk and cheese. Weissberg could care less about the press, or attorneys' egos. In his courtroom, you play by his rules.

Unlike the O.J. fiasco, this would be a speedy, no-nonsense trial, with little time for humor or diversion. In the odd moments during Ardito's trial when there were unavoidable delays, Weissberg would hustle other defendants through, who were seeking court dates for various offenses. After setting a date, he would admonish the defendants that "There is no penalty for showing up early at the courthouse." The humor was ironic—most of those defendants who were not already locked up probably wouldn't show up at all.

The lead attorney for the defense, Franklyn Gould, was a bantam of a man, about 60, and a respected veteran of scores of criminal trials. Jed was lucky to get his firm, Gould, Reimer and Gottfried, to take his case. Unable to afford his own attorney, Ardito had to rely on the court to provide one for him. It turned out to be Gould who, fortunately for Jed, was able to take this "18-B" case. That meant Gould's firm would be paid a fee by the state—$45 per hour—an amount much lower than his normal rate. Whatever the compensation, Gould would not simply go through the motions. He intended to win this case.

His associate was Norman L. Reimer, tall, gray-haired, about the same age as Gould, with the look of a professor. He and Gould usually worked together on major cases.

Across the aisle was Assistant District Attorney Harvey Rosen, an athletic-looking man, about six feet tall, in his forties, with facial hair to compensate for what he was losing on top. It was clear from the beginning that Rosen took the case very personally. He was seeking a conviction for murder in the second degree, and would not even consider a plea. At the conclusion of the trial, when other attorneys in the courthouse flocked to court to hear him give his summation, one was overheard to remark, "Why is Harvey going for murder two? It's a tall order."

But Rosen obviously was convinced that Jed had intentionally killed Marie Daniele, and was determined to prove it. After her homicide, he had naturally been in close contact with the Daniele family and had become friends with them. He knew their loss, and found Ardito's explanation of what had happened outrageous. If Ardito got away with claiming her death was an accident in the midst of kinky sex, every strangler in New York would soon be trying to claim the same defense. It had worked before.

29

Things did not get off to a smooth beginning at the trial, which clearly ruffled Weissberg. Evidence was missing.

The briefcase that Marie Daniele left in the Grand Hyatt the day she was killed had turned up missing. It contained business papers and some personal effects, and it was referred to in court papers, but it had never been examined by the defense.

Gould was furious. It is standard operating procedure for defense attorneys to probe for errors and breaks in procedure by the police. Given the amount of detail that has to be documented, and the numerous procedures that have to be followed, mistakes are not unusual. Sometimes defense attorneys can get evidence thrown out because of those mistakes. They can even have the whole case thrown out.

And that is just what Franklyn Gould tried to do.

"It's a monumental error," he said in an exasperated voice, though he was careful not to raise it. Gould had dealt with Weissberg before.

He maintained that the portfolio could have contained information about the nature of Marie's relationship with Jed before she was killed. It could reflect meetings with

Jed, for example. It would be a lot more reliable, he said, than what she said to friends.

"I move for a mistrial, your honor," said Gould in disgust.

But Weissberg would have none of it. "A new trial won't produce any missing evidence," he said.

It was Frank McDarby who had alerted the defense to the existence of that portfolio. He had sought to examine it, and found out it had been returned to the Daniele family the night of Marie's death, after its contents had been examined by the police in the Midtown South precinct.

The family huddled with the Assistant District Attorney, and someone was dispatched to the Daniele home in Greenpoint, where the portfolio was found and produced in court. It had been placed in Marie's old room.

Its contents proved not very useful, but they did bring the memory of a young, vibrant Marie into the courtroom. The portfolio contained some papers, but also some jelly beans—gifts for her niece?—a pair of sunglasses, and a teddy bear.

The prosecution's case began with police testimony about the crime scene, the taking of photographs and fingerprints, and descriptions of the condition of the deceased and the room's contents. Pretty standard stuff.

In the cross-examination, Norman Reimer peppered Detective Curtis Harris with questions aimed at showing that the crime scene had been compromised. There was a lot of brass present that night, from the chief of detectives on down, and perhaps something had been disturbed. Reimer also wanted to establish that this was not a typical strangulation.

"So there was no sign of a struggle?" Reimer asked, after getting Harris to state the only thing that was apparently disturbed was a bottle of A.1. sauce, which was on its side on the table where Jed and Marie had lunch.

"No," Harris replied.

Reimer also had Harris agree that the body when he saw it, some five or six hours after Marie died, did not show signs of any struggle. Reimer quoted the medical report filled out at the scene, which stated that "The body was found with no apparent sign of trauma."

Harvey Rosen had another chance at Harris, who admitted that the lack of evidence of a struggle did not mean Marie had not been strangled.

Next on the stand was Patrolman William Whelan, who was assigned to the scene, and who also took extensive notes in his memo book. Again, Reimer wanted to show that a lot of police brass had been present. "The hotel room was crowded," Whelan admitted.

Again, the defense moved for a mistrial. There were eight pages of Whelan's memo book that had not been seen by the defense.

The judge again denied the motion, but clearly was exasperated. "I find it extraordinary that this material was not made available beforehand to the defense," he said. But the trial went on.

Denise Marshall then took the stand. She wore a dark dress, a multicolored shawl, and pearls. Her dark red hair was short and curly. She was calm, but obviously anxious to get a lot off her chest. Jed Ardito had played her for a sucker, and she was not amused.

Prior to her testimony, there had been no clear picture of the defendant. He was just some anonymous person who had somehow strangled Marie Daniele. Marshall would fill in the blanks. And the portrait she painted of him was not flattering.

Under Rosen's questioning, she explained that she had known Ardito for about six years, as both a client and a friend. But she claimed, their relationship had always been platonic. She'd been to his apartment a number of times, and he to hers. They'd had dinner, gone to movies, had drinks or coffee.

She'd also known Marie for several years. Rosen honed in on April 1993, the month of Marie's death, when Marshall saw much more of Jed than at any other time during their long friendship.

"She wanted to break up, but he didn't want it to happen," Marshall said. "He was upset about it. He talked about it a lot. He didn't want to stop seeing her."

Marshall described how Jed had come to her office on April 27, and helped himself to money in her bag so he could "buy eyeglasses," and that he had left one of his briefcases in her office by mistake.

"I spoke to him about 9:30 the next day at work. He had me fax him his calendar from the briefcase. I beeped him again about 3, then 3:45. At about 4:30 his office called, saying he'd call about 5:30."

The prosecution's point was clear: With Marie lying dead on the hotel room floor, Jed still thought to call his office. But not 911.

"I arrived home at about 6:30, and got a call from him at 7. He was around the corner, and came by a few minutes later.

"He had on a suit, and an overcoat, but no tie. We had a normal conversation. Then he took a shower, and asked for a bag to go to the drop-off Laundromat. He also asked my sister not to answer the phone.

"About 7:45 we went to the Laundromat. He left his stuff, and we went to the liquor store, then the video store to rent a video, and returned to the house about 8:30. He used the phone—the one in the bedroom—for about an hour. Then he asked for food. I heated some chicken parmigiana. I ordered up Chinese and he asked for some dumplings. At 10:30 we turned on the video—I don't remember what it was. He didn't drink any of the wine we'd bought. Then we went to bed."

"Did you have sexual relations?" Rosen asked.

"No," she insisted.

The following morning, April 29, about 6:30, the phone rang. "Jed answered for a few minutes. I got ready for work. He was lying in bed."

About 8:30, Marshall left her Bay Ridge apartment. "On the way to work, I read an article in the *Daily News*. I panicked. At work I called Eric Goldstein. I asked him to call the police and go and get Jed. I later called Lieutenant [Arthur] Monaghan at Midtown South. The police came to my office, asked some questions, and asked my consent to go to my home."

The courtroom was silent. Throughout her testimony, Ardito had not shown any reaction at all. He simply gazed at Marshall, as if agreeing with her, with no clue as to the impact of what she was saying. She just described how, after killing his girlfriend, Jed had carried on like he was just back from a stroll in the park.

Gould tried to discredit her testimony, by making her out to be lovesick over Jed, a scorned and angry woman with a motive to punish him. After a few questions about how she had been out with Jed and Marie, he asked bluntly:

"Do you love him?"

"No," she said firmly, "not at this time."

"Before?"

"Just as a friend."

Gould then had her acknowledge that Ardito had slept over in her apartment fourteen days during the month of April, but only once before in the six years they had known one another. He even had changes of clothes there.

"Do you have other friends you've slept with, with no sex?" Gould asked.

"Yes," Marshall said, "about three others."

"Did you offer him $500,000 to go to California?"

After hedging about the amount, Marshall agreed she'd made such an offer.

"Were you the least bit jealous of Marie?"

"No," she said.

"Not even after you slept with him for these weeks?" Marshall again said no.

"When you read of her death, did you think you'd lost him forever?"

"No."

"Were you furious?"

"Disgusted would be a good word."

The gallery shared her feelings.

30

When Eric Goldstein was called to the stand, there was a glint of hope in Jed Ardito's eye. He leaned forward just a bit more, he listened a bit more intently, like a student trying to impress his teacher by earnestly paying attention.

Indeed, Goldstein had been Jed's mentor. He'd launched his career, and even backed him in his own office-temp agency. And Goldstein had taken a strong liking to him. He had gone to Jed's wedding to Heather Hughes on the Sarah Lawrence campus in 1985. He even named his son after Jed, despite the practice in the Jewish religion of never naming a child after someone who was still living.

Other prosecution witnesses who knew Jed and Marie had reason to trash him. Denise Marshall had been duped by him, and, as she had testified, was now disgusted with him. Marie's sister, Camilla, naturally had few good things to say about him from the stand. Marie's best friend, Cara Levinson, had never liked Jed, and her distaste for him was obvious when she testified.

Goldstein was caught in the middle. Jed was his good friend, but he had killed Marie, whom he had known, worked with, and liked. He had been like an uncle to both of them.

By his formal manner and speech, Goldstein made it clear he was trying to testify as fairly and objectively as possible. The jury took note.

Rosen asked about Jed's performance on the job. Goldstein seemed eager to reply. "He's the best salesman in New York."

Goldstein was the only witness who had anything positive to say about Jed.

Under Rosen's questioning, Goldstein described how Jed used to come to his Westchester home on Sundays, to spend the day with his family. The last time was two weeks before Marie was strangled. Their conversation, as usual, drifted to the subject of Marie.

"He said he still loved her," Goldstein said. "But she did not wish to marry him."

He went on to describe his involvement in the events of April 28. "I was at home, and got a call from Jed about 8 P.M. He told me Marie was dead. I was shocked. He asked me to call his attorney, which I did. About 8:20, Jed called me back. I told him that his attorney had advised me not to have any conversation with him. All Jed kept on saying was, 'It was an accident . . . it was an accident.' Over and over. I asked him, 'Was it a gun or a knife?' All he said was, 'It was an accident.' "

The next morning, April 29, Goldstein got a call at his office from the police, who still did not know where Jed was. Goldstein told them of the calls he had received from Jed the night before. A few minutes after 9, he got another call from Jed.

"He was beside himself. Incoherent. He didn't know what to do. I told him to pray."

About a half-hour later, Denise Marshall called him, letting Goldstein know of Jed's whereabouts, and Goldstein notified the police. A few hours later Jed was arrested.

Norman Reimer—the "good guy" of the defense team—then questioned Goldstein. He saw a way to score points for his client, even though Goldstein was a witness for the prosecution. Goldstein was obviously reluctant to put nails in Jed's coffin. Reimer had to make the most of that.

Goldstein had described Jed as someone whose honesty was "unimpeachable." He "never lied to me—not even an exaggeration," he stated confidently.

Reimer suspected otherwise. Jed had used Goldstein's credit card to pay for meals at the Hyatt as recently as April of 1993. Because of his financial difficulties, Jed had no credit cards of his own and borrowed Goldstein's card to entertain clients. Reimer wanted to establish that Jed was still seeing Marie, right up to the time of the murder.

Goldstein acknowledged that Marie was still calling Jed in the office during the month of April. He acknowledged that theirs was a "roller coaster relationship," and that he had urged Jed to stop seeing her, as recently as a few days before April 28.

"Did he have lots of Hyatt bills in April?" Reimer asked.

"Yes," Goldstein answered.

"Did you know he was with Marie?"

"No," Goldstein replied.

The next day, Thursday, November 3, there was a discussion out of the jury's hearing about testimony from James LaRossa, Jed's original attorney, who had alerted the police to Marie's death after Jed came to see him. LaRossa was now himself in another courtroom, defending seven members of the Colombo crime family against federal murder charges. He could be subpoenaed to testify, or submit a statement.

"No judge wants to interfere with another judge's trial," Weissberg said, and LaRossa was not required to testify in person.

LaRossa did, indeed, have his hands full. He was up to his ears in yet another a classic mob trial. It featured murder, mob rivalries, alleged mobsters with colorful nicknames—in this case William "Silly Fingers" Cutolo—as well as paid informants and stool pigeons, ratting others out to reduce their own sentences. It was an old-fashioned Mafia trial, and even attracted the interest of columnist Jimmy Breslin.

LaRossa had been hammering at the FBI's use of Gregory Scarpa, a member of the rival Persico gang, as a paid informant. LaRossa painted him as a wild killer against whom his defendants were forced to protect themselves.

LaRossa had a personal reason for wanting to win this case. Early on, the feds had tried to prevent him from even taking the case, charging that he was the Colombo family's in-house counsel. LaRossa fought back, claiming that Scarpa had committed murders while on the FBI's payroll.

The Cutolo trial lasted through that November and right up until a few days before Christmas. It was that timing that clinched Breslin's appearance in the federal courthouse on Foley Square on the last day of the trial. Breslin, no stranger to courtrooms, smelled a Christmas verdict.

"Cutolo's fond wish," Breslin wrote in his column, "is that sometime this week, when the jurors go home, they will pass through the winter night streets ablaze with Christmas lights that reflect on the faces of the happy cheerful people. They will become disgusted at the thought of stool pigeons and be so moved by the lights of the night that they will exclaim, 'Send those men home to their wives and families.'

"In court yesterday, Jimmy LaRossa, the attorney for Cutolo, was remembering a Christmas verdict for an extortionist. . . . 'It was a nullification verdict,' Jimmy said. 'The foreman walked past the defendant and said, "Don't ever do it again."'"

After only two days of deliberation—and with only four more shopping days remaining till Christmas—the jurors found the reputed mob captain and six associates not guilty of all charges. LaRossa and his defendants had gotten a Christmas verdict. Of course, there was more to it than that. But Breslin had his story.

"Merriest Christmas in the world," Cutolo said after the verdict was read. "I've got the best lawyer. This is the best present ever."

Jed Ardito had no such hope of a Christmas verdict—Weissberg would never let the trial last that long. And Ardito didn't have LaRossa in his corner. But things were not looking as grim as they might. His defense team had pretty much established to the jury that Marie had continued seeing Jed during the late winter and early spring of 1993. This countered the prosecution's argument that she had broken off with him and had not seen him for many weeks before Jed lured her to a hotel room, intending to kill her.

Now the defense faced a much more difficult task—getting in the rough-sex defense. It would not be easy without putting Jed on the stand, which could easily backfire on the defense.

The most gruesome part of the trial was coming up—testimony from Dr. Josette Montas, the assistant medical examiner who had performed the autopsy on Marie. Dr. Montas is a Haitian immigrant whose English isn't as polished as it might be. As she testified, she kept watching the time. She was starting her vacation, and was anxious to catch a plane.

Under questioning by the prosecution, she said she performed the autopsy about 10:30 A.M. on April 19, 1993—about the same time Jed was puttering around in Denise Marshall's apartment. She described the finger marks on Marie's neck and the petechial hemorrhaging inside her eyelids and elsewhere on her face—signs of strangulation.

The defense had no choice but to try to tarnish her reputation, try to find mistakes in her procedure. Standard stuff. More important, they had to plant the seed in the minds of the jury that Marie could have strangled in the course of rough sex.

Under cross-examination, the obviously antsy Dr. Montas acknowledged that the body showed no signs of trauma, and that there was no physical evidence of a sexual assault.

And once again the subject of missing evidence was raised—this time some pages from the medical examiner's report, which should have been turned over to the defense attorneys. Once again Franklyn Gould piped up with a request for a mistrial, and once again Judge Weissberg overruled him.

Reimer questioned Dr. Montas about the need to stay current with new medical findings, and brought up research on "modern sexual practices."

"Are all manual asphyxiations characterized as homicides?" he asked.

"Yes," she replied.

He then asked her if she was aware of the number of scholarly articles that had been written, describing the blocking of oxygen to the brain to heighten sexual pleasure. Dr. Montas said she had not read such articles.

Reimer then focused on something which was

described in the medical examiner's autopsy report as a "a small amount of thick white mucus" found in Marie's vagina. There was no evidence of semen found, but Reimer asked Dr. Montas *if the fluid could be seminal fluid*—free of semen—or perhaps fluid generated by the deceased, "consistent with sexual activity."

Dr. Montas stated that the substance could be either of those fluids, but it had not been analyzed.

The defense hoped Dr. Montas had given them the opening they were looking for. If the fluid in Marie's vagina was a result of sex, the prosecution's contention that Jed had murdered her deliberately might come under doubt.

No one realized this more than Harvey Rosen. On redirect, he asked Dr. Montas if the substance found in Marie's vagina could also be a yeast infection. And she agreed that, too, was possible. In short, Dr. Montas could not say exactly what that substance was. Or, more important for the defense, what it was not.

31

Detective Janice Culley knew she would be in for a hard time from the defense. It was par for the course to make cops look like inept bunglers. She also knew they had some ammunition—some things had not been vouchered, such as Marie's briefcase. It had been turned over to the family members, who included a policeman, Steve Cairo. Much would be made of that. Just as much was made of the integrity of the crime scene, simply because a lot of police brass had showed up. Never mind that the scene she and fellow detectives happened upon was totally pristine on the early evening of April 28.

She also knew that she would have to keep her cool on the stand, despite her own strong feelings about the case.

She had been keeping up with the case right through the trial, and knew of the significance of the "thick white mucus" that had been found in Marie's vagina. Assistant District Attorney Rosen had suggested it could be a yeast infection, but he had nothing to back that up.

Between her grillings on the witness stand, Culley went to see Marie's gynecologist, whom Marie had visited several weeks before her death. She was served with a subpoena to testify.

The gynecologist proved to be a reluctant witness. When she appeared in court on Wednesday, November 9, she had her own lawyer in tow. The lawyer claimed she could not be forced to testify, since the information she'd be asked to discuss was privileged information between doctor and patient.

Judge Weissberg was ready for the lawyer. He had been through this before. Piled atop the judge's desk were legal texts, with little sheets of paper marking certain sections of each book.

"This is proper testimony," the judge said testily, alluding to the law books. He criticized the lawyer for not knowing better and reminded him that this was a murder case, and that the medical client was the victim.

Chastened, the attorney took a seat, and the gynecologist took the stand. She testified that her records indicated that Marie Daniele had indeed come to visit her some weeks before her death, complaining about a possible yeast infection. Upon examination, the gynecologist did find a "yeastlike substance," took a swab of it, and sent it out to a lab for analysis. But the test came back negative. Marie thought she had an infection, and so did the gynecologist, but the lab report didn't show it.

There was some discussion over what that all meant, and how such lab tests can often be mistaken. But the weight of evidence seemed to support the Assistant District Attorney's assertion that Marie did, indeed, have an infection, and the infection was the source for the thick white mucus found in her vagina during the autopsy.

The rough-sex defense had suffered a blow. But even more damaging was the ruling by Judge Weissberg. In a discussion with the attorneys, with the jury out of the room, he concluded that thus far in the trial there had not been enough evidence of rough sex to warrant the defense to use it in summation. So far at least, there was nothing to indicate that the death had occurred as an accident during sex.

Franklyn Gould continued peppering Culley with questions about the integrity of the crime scene, and he suggested that she had not followed procedures to the letter. Showing some exasperation at the attacks on her professionalism, Culley did get off a good line that brought smiles to the faces of jurors. When asked if it was a mistake to turn over the portfolio to the family, Culley fired back: "My mistake was allowing the defense attorney to make a mountain out of molehill."

The prosecution's next witness was Dr. Charles S. Hirsch, Chief Medical Examiner of New York City. He was a late entry. The prosecution wanted to bolster its claim that this had been a classic strangulation case. The testimony of Dr. Montas, the Assistant Medical Examiner who had performed the autopsy, had been sullied somewhat. She'd made a mistake in identifying a right and left hand in a photograph which had been presented. It was a minor error, but coupled with her poor English and eagerness to get off the stand and away on her vacation, it might have left the jury with some doubts. So Hirsch, who was Dr. Montas's boss and had checked on the autopsy performed on Marie, was brought in. Not only is Hirsch a very experienced chief medical examiner, he has testified in about 150 murder trials. He is not the type to get rattled by defense lawyers. Not that they didn't try.

Hirsch is a tall man in his late fifties with a long, lean face and an affable manner. It is ironic that a man of his demeanor, who would have a marvelous bedside manner, is a pathologist. The prosecution trotted out his impressive credentials—the places he had been chief medical examiner before, the books and papers he had written, the university affiliations he maintained.

On the stand, Hirsch described in detail how Marie died, and reiterated that she had been strangled for at least two minutes—and was unconscious for at least one minute. He also stated that the seeming evidence of a lack of a struggle did not mean that the Marie had died quietly, nor in the midst of sexual asphyxia. "She could have been quickly overpowered," he said.

Hirsch was patient, calm, serious, and convincing—a prosecutor's dream. He spoke slowly and clearly, and not over the heads of the jurors. When he summed up that Marie died of "manual strangulation," he sounded like Moses.

But Gould had to tarnish his testimony somehow. He brought up one of the books Hirsch had co-written, the *Handbook of Legal Medicine*. It contains a section called "Ten tips for handling yourself in court." Gould wanted to show that Hirsch was an Oscar-winning performer, and not to be swallowed whole. He was very practiced at how to act convincing.

But Hirsch stated calmly he had not written that part of the book, nor edited it. Gould seemed to have attempted a cheap shot, which Hirsch neatly parried.

Gould asked him how many other cases similar to this he had seen. "Many," he replied.

"Would you say it was an ordinary strangulation case?"

"It was typical."

"Nothing startling?" asked Gould, a hint of sarcasm in his voice. He was attempting to suggest that Hirsch might have become jaded at having seen so many strangulation cases, and could no longer tell one from another.

"The only thing startling was how much it was an 'absolute textbook case of manual strangulation,' " Hirsch replied.

Gould then returned to sexual asphyxia, and asked Hirsch if he'd seen the film *Rising Sun*, in which one of the characters dies as a result of the practice. "Did that film particularly interest you?" he asked.

Hirsch didn't bite. "It was a run-of-the-mill movie," he replied innocently.

Gould had not been successful in impeaching Hirsch's testimony in any way. But the Medical Examiner's day in court was not over. On redirect, Rosen asked him about the nature of the "thick white mucus."

"The secretion was not consistent with sexual arousal," Hirsch stated. "The vaginal fluid was white—consistent with a yeast infection. Secretions are colorless."

Hirsch seemed to have slammed the door on the defense. He'd offered a highly credible explanation of how Marie was strangled, and sex had nothing to do with it. The final nail was hammered home when he said that the substance found in Marie's vagina had nothing to do with sex.

But the door had not been shut completely. In fact, Hirsch had given the defense the opening it was looking for. It was Hirsch, the prosecution expert witness, who had first mentioned the term "sexual asphyxia" from the stand.

The defense was now faced with a dilemma: whether or not to put Jed on the stand. On the one hand, he would be able to tell his story. But how convincing would he be? How would the jury react to graphic descriptions of bizarre sexual activity? And most important, how would Jed stand up to Harvey Rosen's cross-examination? Would Rosen be able to get Jed to admit to the February 18 fight, when Marie was heard screaming?

Ardito was a clean-looking young man, now that he had shaved off his beard and came to court dressed like the salesman he was. He was soft-spoken and not easy to rile. And he wanted to testify.

In the end, however, Reimer and Gould decided that

the risk was too great. Especially now that Dr. Hirsch himself had, in effect, introduced the notion of rough sex when he used the term sexual asphyxia. Hirsch had said there was no evidence of it having occurred. But now, at least, the defense could mention it in summation. The defense informed the court that Jed would not testify after all.

The Daniele family—whose members had attended every minute of the trial—was in a relaxed mood. Hirsch had been extremely convincing. The case looked solid. Jed would not testify, which meant they would be spared having to hear his version of Marie's last moments on earth—that she had died in the throes of sexual ecstasy, during kinky lovemaking to which she had consented.

The prosecution, however, showed no such confidence. Rosen knew that Gould would indeed introduce the rough-sex defense in his summation. Prior to Hirsch's testimony, rough-sex had only been alluded to indirectly. Now, it was in—without Jed's testimony. And every district attorney in the country was aware of how that might affect the jury's decision. They all knew of what had happened in the Kathy Holland case a few years earlier on Long Island. It was a rough-sex case over which prosecutors and judges and ordinary citizens still shudder.

32

Who was Kathy Holland, and why did her untimely death have a bearing on Jed Ardito's case? Because the trial of her killer, Joseph Porto, marked the first time the rough-sex defense was used successfully in New York State.

A recap of the case will explain why Harvey Rosen and other prosecutors in strangulation cases fear that defense so much. Its introduction can cause juries to come up with some startling verdicts.

In the fall of 1986, pretty Kathleen Holland was a 17-year-old freshman at the C.W. Post campus of Long Island University. She was a very popular girl who had been a cheerleader at Locust Valley High School, from which she'd graduated the previous June. Friends remember her as bubbly and outgoing.

She had a boyfriend from high school, Joseph Porto, 18, whom friends called sullen and critical.

Friends were puzzled when the pair started going out together in their senior year, and when he took her to the senior prom. Then the friends became concerned. Porto was very possessive of Kathy, even though he was dating other people. He tended to dominate her, had a hot temper, and would sometimes hit her. The relationship was getting dangerous for Kathy, and she wanted to go out with other boys.

But Porto had a tough time accepting the rejection, and on September 27, 1986, using his hands and a graduation tassel, he strangled her to death in the family's Chevy Suburban.

After reporting her missing, and leading police on a wild-goose chase for her, Porto confessed to the murder to police and signed a sworn statement attesting to it. He even repeated his confession on videotape. It was made at 3 A.M., on September 30, three days after Kathy was reported missing.

The videotape shows him walking down a hallway, flanked by police and eating a burger.

Porto, wearing blue jeans and a white top, then sits down, folds his hands, and calmly explains his reason for killing Kathy Holland. He got mad at her because she wanted to date other men. So he strangled her, first with his hands, and then with a graduation tassel. Just like that. But what could have been an open-and-shut case turned out to be the classic rough-sex defense case.

Porto's father Vincent, of Bayville, Long Island, was a realtor and a man of enough means to post $1 million bail for his son, and also to hire the best attorney he could get—Barry Slotnick.

By the time the trial was due to begin, in the spring of 1988, Porto had changed his story. He said his confessions had been lies, and that Kathy Holland had died during a sex act that involved tightening a rope around her neck.

Suddenly, what would have been a sad but relatively quiet trial fell under the media spotlight. Just a few weeks before, Robert Chambers had accepted a manslaughter plea in the highly publicized Yuppie murder case in Manhattan. Chambers had claimed a similar rough-sex defense in strangling Jennifer Levin to death in Central Park. Chambers accepted a plea to manslaughter with a sentence of 5 to 15, years while the jury was deliberating. It was a sentence no one was happy with, least of all the victim's family.

During Porto's trial, Jennifer Levin's father and stepmother arrived in court, to stand by Kathy Holland's parents. "It's the same situation that we've been though," said Steven Levin, the father of the 18-year-old Jennifer. "We've been there, so we just hope we can help."

They couldn't. When Porto took the stand to recant his prior confessions, he sounded like an altar boy. He said that he had accidentally pulled the rope around Holland's neck too hard during the sex act. The only reason he had confessed to murdering her was because he was embarrassed.

On Friday, April 19, 1988, the Nassau County jury acquitted Joseph Porto of murder. They also acquitted him of manslaughter, in the first and second degree. Instead, they found him guilty of criminally negligent homicide, which calls for a maximum of $1\frac{1}{3}$ to 4 years in prison.

The prosecution was stunned. "He coldly and remorselessly confessed to murder and then at trial, he turned on the crocodile tears," said Kenneth Littman, the Assistant District Attorney who tried the case. It was the first time in the history of Nassau County that someone had submitted two confessions and not been convicted.

"It's unfathomable," said Denis Holland, Kathy's father and a retired commander of the Nassau police. "There is something drastically wrong with either the criminal justice system or society itself," he said.

"It's become open season on women," Steven Levin said. "Kill your date, trash her reputation and pay big bucks to get away with murder."

Writing in *Newsday*, Burton C. Agata commented: "The fault is in a readiness to believe incredible stories if they are told by a nice-looking young man about a dead, sexually active young woman. With all the confidence I generally have in the jury system and fully appreciating the need to admit evidence of violent sex, I am still discomfited by the feeling that someone, somewhere, maybe in the courtroom, is thinking, 'Of course, I don't mean that she deserved to die, but. . . .' "

Porto got the maximum, up to four years. Acting County Court Judge John Thorp said that he would "strenuously indicate to the parole board" that Porto not be released from prison until he had served the entire sentence.

There were a number of obvious similarities between the Porto case and the Ardito case. Porto had a prior history of violence with Kathy, as Jed did with Marie. In both cases, the prosecution was not allowed to bring that evidence before the jury.

Porto admitted he killed his girlfriend, as did Jed, and he also claimed, in the end, that the death was an accident, which took place during consensual rough sex.

Porto had to take the stand, to explain away his former confessions, and managed to persuade the jury he was telling the truth. Jed would not take the stand in his case— he had no such prior confessions to recant.

Would the jury in the Ardito case rule the same way as had the Porto jury? It was inconceivable to the Daniele family, who were confident about the case Rosen had presented. They were anticipating a murder conviction.

Experienced court observers, however, were not nearly so confident of that conviction. Juries were never easy to read, and if this one did accept the rough-sex defense, the law weighed heavily in Ardito's favor. You can't convict someone of intentional murder if the death occurred in the throes of passionate lovemaking.

By November 15, 1994, all the principal witnesses in the Ardito case had been heard. It was time for the prosecution and the defense to make ready their summations. The trial soon would be over.

33

In major trials, the summations are like the ninth inning of a baseball game. It's the last time at bat for either side, and a good inning here can determine the game's outcome—especially if the game is close.

There is a little switch made in the last-inning order of things at a trial, however. Normally, the prosecution goes first—in presenting its case and in calling witnesses. But at the summation, the order is reversed and the defense goes first. As in baseball, it's a decided advantage to bat last.

Franklyn Gould was fighting a bad cold, and his voice was weak. Nonetheless, at a few minutes after 10 A.M. on November 15, he addressed the jury for the last time.

He trundled out the "unprofessional behavior of prosecutors," and talked about missing evidence, mishandled property, the crowds of police at the scene. And he said that once the cops found out it wasn't a mob case, they quickly vanished.

He criticized Detective Culley again and again, and then tried to make his client seem unlike the image of a monster painted by the prosecution. Citing the testimony of Marie's sister Camilla and Cara Levinson, he argued that Marie had not stopped seeing Jed, and that their relationship was still very much alive. Jed had invited Marie up to the hotel room not to discuss anything, but simply for "an afternoon of love."

He cited the condoms on the desk and in his bag, and the gift he bought. "Does a murderer buy a gift?" he asked rhetorically.

He suggested that Jed and Marie had an adventurous sex life, and had engaged in "a stupid practice that ended a young life."

Gould tried to demonstrate that Jed was not a violent person. There were some tense moments in the courtroom when he posed this question to the jury: "Did any witness say he was violent?"

This was a sharp stab in the heart of the Daniele family. They knew all too well that Jed had choked Marie before, on February 18, 1993. But the judge would not allow that as evidence. It was bad enough not to be able to show that Jed had choked Marie once before, but now the defense was alleging that Jed was not violent, because no one was allowed to testify about that incident!

Unlike previous occasions when the family felt particularly wronged, there was no audible reaction from the Danieles. But Angie, Marie's mother, lowered her head.

Then Gould attacked the seemingly rock-ribbed testimony of Dr. Charles Hirsch, the Chief Medical Examiner.

Gould argued that the marks on Marie's neck were slight. And that there was no evidence that Marie had grabbed her own neck, in self-defense, an instinctive reaction to being strangled.

Marie did not react that way, he said, because she wasn't being strangled at all.

"Doctor Hirsch called this an ordinary case," said Gould. "A textbook case of strangulation. But if I'm playing with you and you're playing with me . . . and someone dies, is that a classic case?"

Gould used the word "playing" over and over in his summation. Marie and Jed were just playing on the floor. But the image the jury had in their mind of a woman on the floor in that hotel room wasn't playful or sexy. It was the look of death. They had seen pictures of Marie lying there, half clad, with her face swollen and discolored. Gould couldn't eradicate those images.

At 10:59 A.M., Gould finished his summation. His voice fading, weakened by his cold, he sat down. Had he made Jed's case plausible? Had he planted enough seeds in the jury's minds to give them reasonable doubt about the prosecution's charges?

It was now the bottom of the ninth, and it was Harvey Rosen's turn at the plate.

Wearing a dark suit off a discount rack, and a tie to match, Rosen launched his summation. In style, he was all New York—one part Broadway, one part in-your-face basketball. He was a bit edgy, perhaps due to nervousness or anger toward the defendant—and the defense. It didn't matter. It gave a raw edge and a bit of added volume to his voice. No one missed a thing during his summation. News of it had packed the courtroom—his colleagues had come to court to see how he'd do, and perhaps pick up some pointers.

"There are alchemists in history, who said they could turn lead into gold," he began. "That's the defense. Trying to turn murder into an accident."

He went right after Gould's portrayal of Jed as nonviolent, by again showing the jury the shocking picture of Marie taken after her death.

He challenged Gould's explanation of why the couple met at the Grand Hyatt: "It wasn't to have sex but to talk." He claimed Marie agreed to talk there because she knew Jed would get emotional about her rejection of him.

He attacked the suggestion that they had made love at

all. There were no signs of any orgasms. "People don't have orgasms while unconscious." The bed wasn't mussed. They had made a dozen telephone calls in the room. "Is this evidence of any passion?" he asked.

Instead, Rosen charged that Jed strangled Marie and afterward tried to make it look like they had been making love. He suggested that Jed had taken her clothes off afterwards. Rosen mentioned the rolled pantyhose, which Detective Culley had noted at the scene. They were rolled up at the back, which is not the way women remove pantyhose themselves—Jed had removed them.

"And why did he stop undressing her?" Rosen asked. "Because of the gook coming out of her nose!" He was referring to the post-mortem edema, which issued from her face.

"But he didn't call 911," Rosen said. "He called 411," for the number of Jimmy LaRossa. Rosen reiterated how Jed had not surrendered himself, but gone to shower, dine, and spend the evening with another girl—"while Marie is going to the morgue, he has a sit-down dinner."

Jed had been obsessed with Marie, Rosen charged. He constantly pestered her on the phone. Rosen then produced a taped message Jed had left on Marie's answering machine. He played it for the jury, on a tape player he'd brought along for the purpose. On the tape, Jed certainly sounded like a lovesick man who was trying to hang on too long. The message was of the "you'll be sorry I'm gone" variety. "You've lost it totally," Jed remarks at one point. "I think you're weird."

The defense had made much of the fact that the case was built on circumstantial evidence. No one had witnessed the killing. Rosen used another analogy to back the commonsense value of circumstantial evidence. Going to bed on Christmas Eve and waking up with snow on the ground. The evidence it snowed the night before is circumstantial. The defense, Rosen said, would have you believe that it snows in July. In turn, he dealt with most of the defense's points, concluding that they were all so much "snow in July." A nice touch. But he turned back to alchemy for his wind-up.

"No alchemist's brew is going to change murder into an accident. He acted with depraved recklessness and intent. He held her for two minutes." Rosen held up yet again the gruesome picture of Marie. "This is what he acted out."

Removing his watch and placing it on the jury partition, Rosen asked for silence "for two minutes." This must now be standard practice among prosecutors of strangulation cases. Nonetheless, the effect is always dramatic, for the subject is always different.

You tend to picture yourself being strangled for that length of time. Perhaps you hold your breath for a while, to better simulate being strangled. But as the silence goes on, the awareness of how long this is going to take becomes frightening. No one in the courtroom is moving a muscle. The court is as still as a courtroom sketch. The quiet becomes horrifying.

Finally, Rosen picked up his watch. But there is more silence to come. "One minute!" he yelled. Lowered heads shake from side to side. The second minute lasts even longer than the first. And all that time, we have been reminded, Marie was being strangled.

"He took away all her tomorrows because he couldn't accept her decision," Rosen concluded.

After Rosen's "alchemist's brew" soliloquy, Judge Weissberg charged the jury, about 12:40 P.M.

Demanding absolute quiet in the courtroom, and barring anyone else from entering the court lest it break the jury's concentration, Weissberg slowly and carefully explained to the jury the charges they had to consider.

They had four options: murder in the second degree, manslaughter in the first degree, manslaughter in the second degree, and criminally negligent homicide.

Weissberg explained that the jury had to consider each of the charges in descending order, starting with the most serious. Jurors were to first of all consider murder in the second degree. And if they found that charge was not provable, to consider first-degree manslaughter, and so on down the line.

Weissberg then detailed the differences in the charges. To find Jed guilty of murder two, the jurors would all have to agree that Jed had killed Marie with the intent of causing her death. Or, that he had acted out of "depraved indifference to human life"; that he "recklessly created a grave risk of death."

If they could not agree on that crime, they had to consider if Jed had acted "with intent to cause injury, which results in death." That would amount to manslaughter in the first degree.

A notch down was manslaughter in the second degree. One who "recklessly causes the death of another, aware of the substantial risks of death," is guilty of that crime, the judge explained.

The final option was criminally negligent homicide, which would mean that the jury would have to find that Jed had not meant to cause any harm to Marie. Such a finding would mean the jury bought the defense's claim that Marie's death was a tragic accident.

Depending on how they found—not guilty of all the charges was not a realistic hope for him—Jed could be sentenced to anything from a few months in prison, on up to 25-years-to-life. With his future in their hands, the jurors went off to lunch, and then to deliberate.

Jed Ardito was taken back to jail. During the trial, he had been staying at the Brooklyn Men's Correctional

Center, not Rikers Island. He was fortunate. There was trouble again at Rikers Island. The inmates had gone on a hunger strike. If he'd been returned there, he would have had no dinner that evening. Someone awaiting a murder verdict might be excused for not having much of an appetite. But Jed didn't like to miss any meal. He had eaten heartily the night he killed Marie Daniele, on April 28, 1993. The jurors who would decide his fate had been reminded of that early and often by the prosecution.

34

The jury did not deliberate long. The lunch they had in the courtroom on November 15, moments after being charged by Judge Weissberg, was the last meal they would have to eat at the courthouse.

The jurors deliberated for a few hours that afternoon before going home for the evening. The jury was not sequestered, an act of consideration on the part of the judge which had to be approved by the defendant. The judge asked him directly, "Mr. Ardito, do you have any objection?"

Jed was a bit startled by the question. It was the first time during the entire trial that any deference at all was paid the defendant. He was being asked cordially, by the people who could wind up putting him away for the best years of his life, for a favor. Ardito quickly shook his head. "No, I have no objection, your honor."

It's no little thing—allowing the jury to go home at the end of the day and be with their families instead of having to hole up in a hotel and eat institutional food with relative strangers until a verdict is reached. And trials are all about the accumulation of things in one's favor. Certainly, the Daniele family was not pleased that the judge or jury should owe any debt of gratitude to the man who had strangled their Marie—especially right at the moment they would begin deciding his fate.

As it turned out, any sequestration would have lasted only one night, anyway, even though there were a lot of options for the jury to consider, and much room for debate. But before noon the next day, November 16, the jurors sent word to the judge that they had reached a unanimous verdict. They had deliberated only a few hours. The defense braced. A quick verdict is usually a guilty verdict.

As the jurors returned, the atmosphere in the courtroom was markedly different from what it had been during the trial. During the weeks before, jury and spectators had been lulled by the rhythm of the proceedings. It was as if they were watching a tennis match, with the judge as referee. First, each side got to score an ace—an unreturned shot, during their opening arguments. Then the game began in earnest. The prosecution served first, presenting its witnesses. The defense returned with cross-examination. There was volleying with additional questioning. There were tactical displays—sidebars and objections and requests for mistrial.

On and on the game went, sometimes fascinating, sometimes heartbreaking, sometimes boring. But the tension between attorneys never ceased. They were the stars, on court, doing their thing.

It was easy to forget what was at stake, and what the trial was all about. But no longer. Not as the verdict was to be announced. The lawyers were no longer on center court. They, too, were now relegated to being spectators. Even the judge took a back seat. All eyes now focused on the jury as they shuffled into the room. They were now the stars. They would determine who had won this deadly game.

The courtroom was packed. The Daniele family, as

usual, was well represented. Ralph Daniele, the father of the victim, fixed his gaze on the back of Jed Ardito's head. If looks were a hatchet, Ardito would have been decapitated.

Jed's expression was little different from what it had been during the entire course of the trial. There was no fear in his face, no arrogance, no feigned humility. At no time during the trial had he expressed much emotion at all, except curiosity. He'd seemed most interested in the testimony of two witnesses, Eric Goldstein and Denise Marshall, who had both known him well. Jed listened keenly to what they thought of him, as if that could possibly matter any longer. Jed would soon be out of their lives forever, no matter the verdict. But Jed obviously liked hearing about himself through the eyes of others—just as long as he was the center of attention.

At no time did he come close to breaking up over Marie. She was history to him now. Any grief he might have felt had disappeared as he sat in jail awaiting trial, trying to figure out how to save his skin. He never had to look away or shield his eyes with his hands when photos of Marie's lifeless body were displayed. He didn't react when the tape of her voice, pleading for help, was played in the courtroom during the pretrial hearing. He did not smile when the rare funny moment arose—as several inevitably do during a trial, welcomed moments of comic relief. He did not tighten his jaw muscles or show anger when Assistant District Attorney Harvey Rosen called him a cold-hearted murderer.

It was as if he, too, were just a visitor here, and that someone else was on trial, some other Jed Ardito.

The Daniele family had been cautioned by the judge a few times during the trial, because they had audibly expressed disgust or disbelief at comments made by the defense attorneys. Ralph Daniele had even been asked to leave the courtroom. After that incident, the family managed to contain its reactions and words for outside the courtroom.

But not this time. When the words "Not guilty" were read to the charge of murder in the second degree, the Ardito family erupted. How could he not be guilty? He'd strangled her with his own hands!

"You should rot in hell!" one member of the family screamed at Ardito. "You will have your day!"

The judge angrily tried to restore order. The tumult caused Jed to turn around from his defendant's chair. It was the first time during the entire trial that he faced members of the family that had once welcomed him with such open arms, people who would have been his own family. One who would have been a brother-in-law shouted at him, "Don't you turn around! Don't you look at me, Buddy!"

The judge thought it prudent to order two armed escorts for the defense attorneys.

But of course Jed was not off the hook by a longshot. He had been spared the sentence of 25 years to life, but still faced the possibility of plenty of hard time.

If found guilty of first-degree manslaughter, Jed faced 8⅓ to 25 years.

Another option was second-degree manslaughter, which would mean a sentence of 5 to 15 years. That was the sentence which Robert Chambers had plea-bargained for in his rough-sex case.

But if he were only found guilty of criminally negligent homicide, the sentence could be as little as two more years in prison.

After the judge settled down the courtroom, the rest of the verdict was read. To the charge of manslaughter in the first degree, the jury found the defendant "Guilty."

A sigh of relief filled the room. At least he wasn't going to be free any time soon.

There was a lot of latitude allowed Judge Franklin Weissberg in sentencing Jed on December 12. If the judge recommended Jed serve the minimum 8⅓ years, he'd be out of prison in his early forties. But if Jed had to spend the maximum 25 years in prison, he'd be near 60 when he got out. What would this handsome, dark-haired young man look like in the year 2018? Would he be gray-haired, with a bit of a paunch and a thousand-mile stare in his eyes? With a quarter-century of hard time behind him, he would be a very different man. But he would still be alive. Marie Daniele would have been dead over 25 years, more than she'd lived.

Judge Weissberg thanked the jury—he had been courteous to them throughout. Jed was led away. The armed guards ushered out the defense attorneys. The trial was over, but not the reaction to it.

The Daniele family's outrage resonated with parents of young girls everywhere and with women's groups. And the press covered that reaction on radio, television, and print. Of course the media played up the rough-sex angle, even though the term "rough sex" had never even been uttered in the formal course of the trial. And it was clear that the rough-sex question could not have weighed heavily on the minds of jurors, if at all. For one thing, the verdict had been swift, allowing little time for much debate over the issue. More important was the precise verdict which the jurors reached—guilty of manslaughter in the first degree. That meant the eleven women and one man had determined Jed had meant to harm Marie when he grabbed her in the hotel room, and in doing so had caused her death. They could never have reached that verdict if they believed her death was due to an accident during lovemaking.

The *New York Post* went to "the wood"—the front page—with the story. The headlines screamed:

FUROR OVER
ROUGH
SEX
VERDICT

There were pictures of Marie Daniele and Jed Ardito. She looked radiant and pretty, a studio photograph from the family. The caption under her head shot read: "Strangled in midtown hotel room by lover Gerald Ardito."

He looked distant and stunned in a press photo taken after his arrest. The caption under his photo read: "Used rough-sex defense to beat murder charge." There was also a sub-headline: "Millionaire beats murder charge." Jed Ardito didn't have two nickels to rub together.

Both the *Post* and the *Daily News* quoted Angie Daniele: "It was an abortion of justice. The judge handcuffed the prosecutor," she said, referring to the inadmissibility of the 911 evidence.

Women's rights supporters also expressed outrage. "It means batterers who use rough sex as a defense can get away with murder," said the director of the Center for Battered Women's Legal Services. The president of New York's National Organization for Women said, "[The tape] clearly would have had an impact on a jury's verdict."

Judge Weissberg had four weeks to consider just how long Jed Ardito would be incarcerated. The pressure on him to give the maximum was only starting to build.

35

Jed Ardito was sentenced on December 12, 1994. The courthouse was girdled with court officers—18 in all, including one giant of a man who held ground at the velvet rope. Sentencings can bring out the worst in families and friends of victims.

But the Danieles needed no guards, they needed only a few minutes of the court's time. Angela Biondo, one of Marie's sisters, read a statement explaining how much Marie would be missed, how much she was loved, how much she would have enjoyed her new nieces.

The statement went on to disparage the court for not allowing in the 911 evidence, and for allowing the defense to infer Jed was not violent.

It was both a lament for Marie and a critique of the judge, but was more eloquent than relevant. The judge's mind had long since been made up. And despite what the family thought—that Weissberg was somehow pro-Ardito, since he'd banned the 911 tape—the judge demonstrated he held no brief at all for the defendant.

Before reading the specific sentence, Weissberg stated that he had received some 26 letters asking leniency for the defendant. But they had no effect at all on his sentence. He looked down from the bench at Ardito, no longer bothering to conceal his contempt. He told Ardito his actions were "cold, calculating and utterly devoid of remorse."

Weissberg also cited Jed's early, abortive attempt to plead insanity. "It was a transparent and incompetent attempt to fool the court," he said. Weissberg then read the sentence, 8⅓ to 25 years, and added his own recommendation—that Jed not be paroled, and be required to serve the maximum sentence, 25 years.

There was applause in the courtroom, and the Daniele family hugged one another, as Jed was led away in handcuffs. The man who would have been one of their own would now have a different family for perhaps a quarter of a century. They shouted at the "snake in an Armani suit," as one relative had dubbed him. "Rot! Rot! Rot!" they shouted. "I hope you die in there!"

As of this writing, Jed is appealing his conviction.

Reporters and camera crews crowded around family members outside on the courthouse steps. The Daniele ordeal was over, and at least Ardito had been given the maximum the law allowed for manslaughter. But they will never be satisfied.

"A life for a life," said Marie's father. "But I don't think he'll ever get out."

Frank McDarby was asked his thoughts. "Harvey [Rosen] said all you can say," he said. "The jury has spoken. Justice is a witches' brew."

Then he reflected a moment, and recalled what Rosen had said of Gould's summation. "It's a witches' brew, but not an alchemist's brew."

AMY FISHER—VICIOUS KILLER OR VICTIM OF LOVE?

THE ELECTRIFYING CASE THAT INSPIRED THE BLOCKBUSTER TV MOVIE!

While her Long Island high school classmates happily planned dates for the prom, 17-year-old Amy Fisher appalled them with tales of her wild sexual escapades, of her steamy, obsessive alleged affair with a married man— of a wife she wanted out of the picture.

But it wasn't until Amy was arrested for attempting to slay unsuspecting Mary Jo Buttafuoco in cold blood in front of her own home, that police and reporters uncovered Amy Fisher's hidden world—a world that included secret call girl rings, attempts to hire hitmen with payment in sex—and a beeper still nestled in her purse on which clients could page her with personal codes.

LETHAL LOLITA

by Maria Eftimiades

Lisa Steinberg—six years old and defenseless, she was the brutalized victim of a couple's descent into delusion and violence.

Joel Steinberg—cruel and controlling, he ruled his family with intimidation and a deadly iron fist.

Hedda Nussbaum—beaten and brainwashed, did her loyalty to Joel keep her from saving Lisa—or was there a more disturbing reason?

Never before has a trial been so shocking, nor testimony so riveting. Here for the first time is the entire heart-rending story of an outwardly normal family living in the shadow of violence and fear, and the illegally adopted, innocent girl whose life was the price of affection. Retold in the framework of the sensational trial, it is a sad and gripping tale that stabs at the heart's tenderest core.

Documented with 8 pages of gripping photographs

LISA, HEDDA & JOEL
The Steinberg Murder Case

Newlyweds Pam and Gregg Smart seemed like the perfect American couple. He was an up-and-coming young insurance executive, she the beautiful former cheerleader who now worked in the administration of the local school.

But on May 1, 1990, their idyllic life was shattered when Gregg was murdered in the couple's upscale Derry, New Hampshire townhouse—a single shot to his head. Three months later, the grieving widow was arrested and charged with the brutal crime.

In the dramatic trial that followed, a dark portrait of Pam Smart emerged—one of a cold manipulator who seduced a high school student with a striptease and then had a wild affair with him—until he was so involved with her that he was willing to do anything for her...even murder...

DEADLY LESSONS

BY EDGAR AWARD NOMINEE
KEN ENGLADE